Guide to the MALDIVES

•

LYDIA J. CUTHBERTSON

Guide to the Maldives, first edition
Text copyright © 1994 Lydia J. Cuthbertson

Photographs, black and white copyright © Lydia J. Cuthbertson
Photographs, cover and colour section © Elizabeth Wood

All rights reserved

Layout and cover design: Jane Stark
Typesetting, maps and diagrams: Johan Hofsteenge

A CIP catalogue record for this book is available from the British Library
ISBN 0 907151 80 9

Also published by IMMEL Publishing:
Fishes of the Maldives	John E. Randall
Red Sea Reef Fishes	John E. Randall
Tropical Marine Life	Dieter Eichler
Red Sea Safety	Peter Vine
Red Sea Invertebrates	Peter Vine
Sharks of Arabia	John E. Randall

Immel Publishing Limited
20 Berkeley Street
Berkeley Square
London WIX 5 AE
Tel: 071 491 1799 Fax: 071 493 5524

CONTENTS

Introduction 7

General Information 9
- Geography 10
- History and People 12
- Tourism 15
- Airport Procedure 19
- Currency and Payments 21
- Electricity 23
- Flora and Fauna 10
- Agriculture 13
- Entry Requirements 18
- Transport 20
- Dress 22
- Medical Advice 23

Diving 29
- Background Information 30
- Fish Feeding 36
- Dive Prices 38
- Choosing an Island Base 41
- Marine Hazards 60
- Reefs 32
- Dive Certificates 37
- Diving Practices 39
- Dive Sites 44

Resorts 69
- Introduction 70
- A-Z resorts 72

Appendices 119
- Helicopters 120
- Useful addresses 123

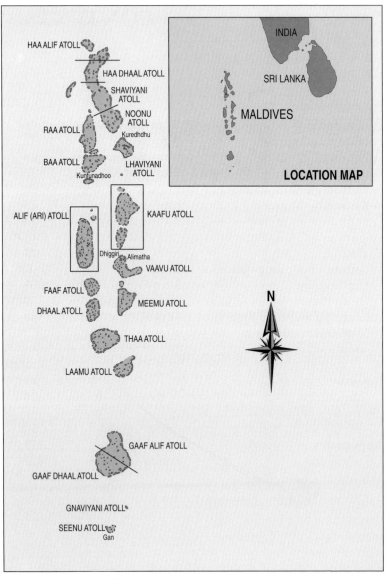

The Republic of Maldives.

INTRODUCTION

The first glimpse most people have of the Maldives is a breathtaking aerial view of sparkling sand-fringed coral atolls set in an aquamarine sea.

These curiously shaped islands originate from volcanic eruptions which occurred deep below the sea when the earth's crust cracked and spread, creating volcanic hot spots. Escaped molten lava gradually formed sub-peaks. Mountain chains grew and eventually rose from the seabed to the surface, shaping islands which are like icebergs, tiny scraps of land perched on top of subsea mountains, constantly changing and evolving. Barely rising above high-tide level, the islands have a precarious existence, at risk from both erosion and sea-level rise.

Frequent rain penetrates the soft porous limestone bedrock, forming a freshwater lens beneath the surface of the islands, sustaining plant life above and preventing seawater from seeping inwards. However, despite readily available freshwater the range of land-based flora and fauna is somewhat limited. But this is amply compensated for by the extraordinary variety of marinelife on the spectacular coral reefs that surround the islands. It is this marine richness which makes the Maldives so popular with divers. The magnificent natural setting, an ample supply of sunshine and a well-deserved reputation as a wonderful place to relax, also attract less adventurous tourists.

8 *Guide to the Maldives*

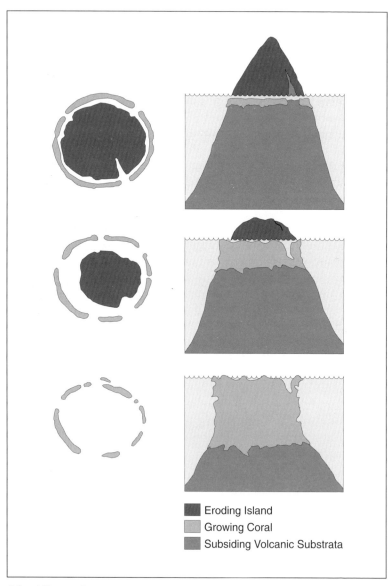

Island Formation.

GENERAL INFORMATION

Local fishing dhonis - Biyadoo. Larger motorised versions are used for guests on organised fishing trips.

Geography
Flora and Fauna
History and People
Agriculture
Tourism
Entry Requirements
Airport Procedure
Transport
Currency and Payments
Dress
Electricity
Medical Advice

GEOGRAPHY

The Republic of Maldives is an archipelago of 1,190 small coral islands on the Indian Ocean, of which 202 are inhabited. The islands are formed into 26 natural atolls, rings of land surrounding tropical lagoons, which are in turn surrounded by a coral reef. For administrative purposes the islands are divided into 20 units, also called 'atolls'. The total area, including land and sea is about 90,000 sq. km (35,000 square miles). The length of the archipelago is 823 km (500 miles) and it is 130 km (81 miles) at its greatest width. Its nearest neighbours are India and Sri Lanka situated about 600 km (375 miles) and 670 km (415 miles) to the north and east respectively.

The coral reef surrounding each atoll has several deep natural channels serving as entry points for vessels. The islands are very small and low-lying; most are no more than 3 m above sea level. There are no rivers or lakes in the Maldives, although some of the larger islands have depressions in the centre where freshwater gathers. Common features are tall coconut palms, white sandy beaches and crystal clear aquamarine lagoons.

The average annual rainfall is 1967 mm (77 inches). The mean daily maximum temperature is 30°C (86°F), and the mean daily minimum 26°C (79°F).

FLORA AND FAUNA

By gentle waves and monsoon storms, sand and coral rubble is piled onto the Maldives' shores forming shifting banks, which are bound and stabilised by salt-tolerant shrubs and grasses. Mangrove areas are found on many shores and unlike other stabilising plants, they grow where their roots are constantly bathed in seawater. Mangroves benefit islands by helping to protect the shores from erosion and they benefit the reefs by trapping silt and providing valuable sheltered breeding areas for many fish and invertebrates.

Some creepers such as *Ipomea* - sea morning glory - or shrubs such as *Scaevola* and *Tournefortia* live at high-tide mark and above. As they increase in density, their leaf litter, together with the droppings of nesting birds and roosting fruit bats, add organic nutrient to the soil and sand, replacing some of that which is washed away by rain. Beach and land crabs dig tunnels and continuously mix leaf litter through the sand in a similar manner to earthworms.

The sandy soil restricts the variety of plants that can flourish but constant fertilisation, using cow manure imported from India and Sri Lanka, encourages some beautiful and spectacular growths such as the beach *naupaka* and the wonderfully scented *frangipani* or temple flower which wafts its strongest scent at night. Hibiscus flowers in profusion.

The lovely Frangipani *or temple flower.*

The coconut palm is also prominent and an important crop as it can produce juice, flesh for eating, cooking oil, fibre for making ropes and wood for building boats. Some islands also grow bananas which are very small but extremely rich and tasty.

The Maldives are not noted for their wildlife, but reef herons are common and occasionally pairs of white fairy terns are seen. There are a few small rodents. Reptiles are abundant, lizards frequently scurry through the undergrowth. Less easy to observe are the well-camouflaged long-tailed chameleons that live in trees. After dark, geckos, small golden reptiles, attach themselves to walls of buildings using their splayed feet as suction pads. These are friendly-looking creatures who perform a valuable service since they feed on insects and help to control mosquitoes.

HISTORY AND PEOPLE

Archaeological finds reveal that the Maldives were inhabited as early as 1500 BC, but the first known settlers were Aryan immigrants who came to the islands around 500 BC. Throughout history the islands provided safe anchorages for travellers from east and west. Trading contacts with Arabs, Persians, Malaysians, Indonesians and Chinese left their imprints on the people and culture of the country. Modern Maldivians are a mixed race, some displaying prominent Aryan features, others looking more Dravidian, Arab or Negroid, but their exact origin still remains unknown.

With the exception of a fifteen year period (1558-1573) when the Portuguese invaded from their colony in Goa, the Maldives has remained an independent sovereign state. However, in 1887 when Britain was the all-powerful force in the Indian Ocean, an agreement was formalised whereby the country became a British protectorate. Through this arrangement, the Maldives retained uninterrupted links with Sri Lanka, on whom it was so heavily dependent for all manner of supplies. The close connection with Britain continued during the Second World War when the island of Gan, in the southerly Addu atoll, served as an important RAF staging post under an agreement with Britain that was terminated in 1976.

The Maldives assumed full independence in 1965, becoming the 133rd member of the United Nations and the smallest nation in South East Asia. The form of government changed from a sultanate to a republic on 11 November 1968. Under the present constitution, the President is nominated by the Citizen's Majilis (Parliament) and elected by vote for a term of five years.

Arab traders introduced Islam in 1153 AD, until then

Buddhism had been the dominant religion. Islam is now the state religion and the backbone of society. The vast majority of the population are Sunni Moslems. Dhivehi, the national language, belongs to the Indo-Iranian group, but also shows a strong Arabic influence. Its script, introduced in the late sixteenth century, is written from right to left.

The population in 1990 was estimated at 2,141,139 of which 56,060 lived in the capital, Male. Because of the problems of overcrowding in the capital, certain islands which had been designated as tourist resorts are now being handed back to the Maldivians.

The Government has resolved to keep the tourists away from Maldivian society as much as possible to avoid the latter being corrupted by Western ways. Therefore it is extremely difficult for independent travellers to visit those islands which are not designated resort areas.

AGRICULTURE

Agriculture occupied an important place in the economy of the Maldives in the recent past. Its role was reduced for some time due to change in food habits and because of opportunities in other sectors, which produced a higher income. The Government, however, realises the value of agriculture and is taking steps to provide a place for it in the island's development. Incentives are being offered with a view to encourage Maldivians to look to agricultural activities to provide employment. Some of the uninhabited islands are being leased for the cultivation of coconut and other high-value crops and for developing poultry farming. Land-reform legislation is under serious consideration to provide security of tenure for entrepreneurs.

The significance of the coconut tree in the economy of the Maldives throughout history can be seen in the fact that it is called *Dhivehi ruh*, which means 'the Maldivian palm'. Coconut is the most important agricultural product of the islands.

Coconuts and coconut products form an integral part of the people's diet and coconut timber is widely used for boatbuilding and construction purposes. In the present administration programme in the archipelago, president Maumoon Abdul Gayoom's call for the citizens of the country to plant a coconut tree each has received wide support from all sections of the population.

Other crops include arecanut, betel vines, (betel chewing is very popular) cereals, (a Maldivian staple, *roshi* is prepared from millet flour) cassava, taro, alocasia, sweet potatoes and vegetables, mainly for domestic consumption, as well as a wide variety of tropical and subtropical fruits, both for domestic consumption and to serve the tourist industry.

Poultry farming is at present a household activity, with birds being reared in back gardens. There is, however, one large poultry farm in one of the uninhabited islands which relies on imported chicks and feed. Since the eggs and poultry meat

Fallen coconuts after a storm.

produced in the Maldives are insufficient for local demand, and substantial quantities are imported every year, the Ministry of Fisheries and Agriculture has established an incentives programme with the aim of achieving self-sufficiency in these products.

TOURISM

Their extraordinary natural beauty makes the Maldives special for many visitors. However, despite the great potential for tourism, it is still a relatively young tourist destination. The first resort was developed in 1972, on an uninhabited island near Male. Known as Kurumba village, it only had accommodation for about 60 guests. The second resort was Bandos, with about 280 beds. Food was mainly restricted to local produce and transport quite slow. At that time air travel to the Maldives was only available on Air Ceylon (now Air Lanka) which operated a small Avero aeroplane. This carried only 48 passengers and took two hours to reach the Maldives from Colombo. Despite all these constraints, more than a thousand pioneer tourists came to the islands in 1972.

Tourism furnishes more foreign exchange than any other economic sector. It provides more than a quarter of the government's revenue. In 1989 more than US$70 million was earned from tourism alone compared to US$49.5 million in 1987. It ranks second among the main industries, behind fishing and ahead of shipping.

In 1978 President Gayoom agreed an open policy on domestic and foreign investment in tourism, and a law regulating the industry was passed in 1979. To strengthen the existing organisational structure, a separate department for tourism was created in 1982, which became a ministry in 1988. A Tourism Advisory Board was formed in 1984 to act as a consultative body. Thus tourism developed from an unchecked and unplanned economic activity to a carefully monitored and regulated industry.

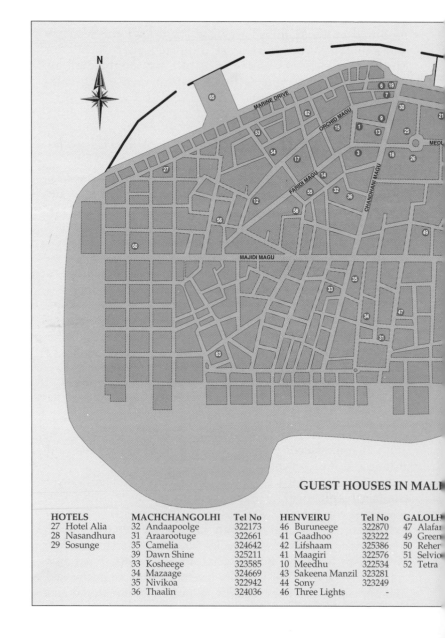

GUEST HOUSES IN MALE

HOTELS	MACHCHANGOLHI	Tel No	HENVEIRU	Tel No	GALOLH
27 Hotel Alia	32 Andaapoolge	322173	46 Buruneege	322870	47 Alafar
28 Nasandhura	31 Araarootuge	322661	41 Gaadhoo	323222	49 Green
29 Sosunge	35 Camelia	324642	42 Lifshaam	325386	50 Reher
	39 Dawn Shine	325211	41 Maagiri	322576	51 Selvio
	33 Kosheege	323585	10 Meedhu	322534	52 Tetra
	34 Mazaage	324669	43 Sakeena Manzil	323281	
	35 Nivikoa	322942	44 Sony	323249	
	36 Thaalin	324036	46 Three Lights	-	

MAP OF MALE

LOCATIONS

AIRLINES
Air Maldives	2
Air Lanka	4
Alitalia	
Austrian Airways	4
Balair	3
Condor	4
Indian Airlines	8
LTU, LTS	5
Lauder Air	61
Monarch Air	3
Sterling Airways	3
Singapore Airlines	1
Pakistan Int. Airlines	4
Emirates	28
Interflug	2

BANKS
Bank of Ceylon	7
Bank of Credit & Commerce	30
Bank of Maldives Ltd.	8
Habib Bank	9
Maldives Monetary Authority	6
State Bank of India	10

CONSULATES & EMBASSIES
U.S.A.	11
Bangladesh	12
France	13
Germany	14
India	15
Pakistan	16
Sri Lanka	17

TELECOMMUNICATION
Dhiraagu	18
Post Office	19

EMERGENCY SERVICES
Hospital	20
Police	21

GOVERNMENTS OFFICES
Atolls Administration	2
Civil Aviation Authority	2
Customs	65
Foreign Affairs	22
Immigration & Emigration	23
Information & Broadcasting	23
Ministry of Tourism	24
Tourist Information Unit	22

PLACES OF INTEREST
Islamic Centre	25
National Museum	26

	MAAFANNU	Tel No
Tel No	54 Dheraha	323018
-	55 Ever Pink	324751
322279	56 Fehividhuvaruge	324470
-	53 Kaimoo Stop Over Inn	323241
324671	58 Maafaru	322220
323305	60 Male Tour Inn	326220
	59 Mermaid Inn	323329
	61 Ocean Reed	323311
	62 Shabnamge	-
	63 Velagali	322267

Tourism promotion is now carried out jointly by the Government and the private sector. The Government and local resort operators participate in all major international fairs, and attend exhibitions in key markets. Before the Government began its promotional activities, the main tourist market for the Maldives was Western Europe. The number of visitors arriving from here has grown steadily ever since the beginning of tourism. Although Germans and Italians still top the tourist arrivals, Japan has become the fastest-growing market: it has moved from ninth position in 1983 to third place today. In 1985 alone there was a doubling of arrivals from both Japan and Australia. An important local association for the promotion of tourism is the Maldives Association of Tourism Industries (MATI).

ENTRY REQUIREMENTS

Almost all visitors to the Maldives arrive by air. Male International Airport is situated at Hulhule island just 1.5 km (1 mile) or 10 minutes by boat from Male. A valid passport is required for entry. In addition, an international certificate of inoculation against yellow fever is needed if coming from a place that is infested. Foreigners who enter the Maldives must be in possession of at least US$10 per day of their stay, unless they are coming with a tourist agency or on recruitment. Indians, Pakistanis, Bangladeshis and Italians are given a 90-day entry permit on arrival. All other tourists except Sri Lankans are given a 30-day permit. This can be extended for a nominal fee. Sri Lanka passport holders are not allowed to visit the Maldives.

It is advisable that all visitors have confirmed hotel reservations in the Maldives since this information is required for immigration clearance. However, any visitor entering the Maldives without a confirmed hotel reservation can seek assistance from the airport tourist information counter.

AIRPORT PROCEDURE

Hulhule island is just enough to accommodate a runway and the terminal building. Although ticket destinations read 'Male', visitors will need to arrange an excursion from one of the resorts if they wish to see the capital. Independent travellers can arrange ferry crossings from the airport by contacting the airport tourist information counter.

On arrival at Hulhule airport, after passing through customs, visitors are met by representatives of the various islands and gather in groups. At this point they hand over their tickets to the island representatives. The tickets are required because flights have to be confirmed at least three days before the return journey and they are returned when the travellers are met again at the airport on their return from the resort. Passengers will not be permitted to enter the airport terminal until they are in possession of their flight tickets.

In 1991 baggage trolleys were introduced at the baggage carousel, enabling visitors to wheel their baggage to the customs desks, where it is opened and searched, mainly for alcohol and literature or pictures that are considered offensive to these Islamic people. The airport is not air-conditioned and can be extremely hot and humid throughout the year. Baggage trolleys certainly make life a lot easier and are a vast improvement on the previous system of porters. It is no longer necessary to have US dollar notes ready to tip the countless porters who used to operate independently outside the terminal building. Luggage can now be wheeled to and from the various jetties, where it is loaded and off-loaded on to the boats.

Before leaving the Maldives and before checking in at the airport a departure tax of US$7 is payable. It is easier if the correct denomination is to hand. If not, there is a currency exchange desk in the main check-in hall.

Queues of departing passengers entering the terminal building are generally long. Once inside and checked in, passengers can use the restaurant/cafeteria which leads out on to a thatch-shaded terrace. No alcohol is served or available to be consumed on the airport island, and food and beverages are expensive in comparison to the resorts. There are a few shops next to the restaurant offering an interesting selection of souvenirs including books, clothing, jewellery, postcards and sundries.

TRANSPORT

There is no centralised transport between the islands. The most common mode of transport is by local boats called *dhonis*, sturdy wooden vessels with canvas canopies overhead. Their usual speed is about 13kph (8mph). Many operate as ferries between Male and the airport. Tourist resorts have their own transfer boats, in some cases high-powered speed boats. Once a

Hummingbird helicopter taking off from Rasdhu helipad.

reservation is confirmed the resorts and hotels send their representatives to the airport to meet their clients.

Hummingbird Helicopters operate services for transport, sight-seeing and away-day diving trips. Tickets are not usually supplied in advance but are issued at the Hummingbird office immediately outside the main door of the airport terminal. Passengers are taken to the helipad a short distance from the terminal building in an unmistakable yellow tractor and trailer with overhead canopy. Although helicopter travel is noisy, this is an ideal way to gain a bird's eye view of the islands.

CURRENCY AND PAYMENTS

Major currencies may be exchanged at the local banks, leading shops and tourist resorts. When changing foreign funds into Maldivian money no restrictions apply. However, when leaving the country, only 10 per cent of what was converted on arrival may be reconverted, and it is essential to produce the original bill of exchange. The unit of Maldivian currency is the rufiya, which is subdivided into 100 larees. Coins in use are 1, 2, 5, 10, 20 and 50 larees and 1 rufiya. The American dollar is the most common foreign currency in use, although payments at the resorts can be made in most major foreign currencies, as well as by travellers' cheques or credit cards. The most frequently used credit cards are American Express, Visa, Mastercard, Diners Club and Eurocard.

Guests wishing to settle their bills by credit card should inform reception staff upon arrival. Some resorts have been known to add a surcharge of up to 5 per cent on bills paid by credit card.

On the resort islands, all drinks, additional meals to half- or full-board reservation, items bought from the souvenir shop, watersports and excursions are signed for. The total bill must be settled the night before departure. Depending on the policy of the resort, if a minibar is provided with the room, this may be cleared of all stock at least 24 hours before departure. It is worth arranging with reception on the day of departure for sufficient drinks and snacks to cover for any waiting around between room vacation and pick-up.

DRESS

With the high humidity in the Maldives, light cotton clothing is recommended. Nudity is forbidden. When visiting an inhabited island or the capital, shorts and tee-shirts for men, and blouses or tee-shirts and skirts or shorts that cover the thighs (made of non-diaphanous material) for women, are the minimum requirements. On resort islands dress is casual and sporty. Men and women can wear very little clothing if they wish and comfortably stroll around their island in brief swimwear. In the restaurants and cafeterias, out of respect to the staff, it is polite for men to slip on a vest to cover their torso and women to put on a tee-shirt or shift that skims the thighs if they prefer to keep their swimwear on.

Since evenings can be quite cool, some warmer clothing should be brought.

Most paths at the resorts are of sand and coral rubble. Occasionally footpaths are reinforced with intermittent concrete slabs. In any event, it is advisable to have flat comfortable shoes for strolling around the island and some plastic or rubber sandals for the beach. A sturdy pair of plastic shoes or diving boots is essential for walking out to the reef edge at low tide. They should be well fitting and have tough soles and heels, preferable serrated for grip since the rocks and coral can be extremely slippery.

I have never actually seen any sun hats for sale in the Maldives and would recommend that you bring your own. Baseball caps are best, they are cool, have a good peak to protect the eyes and most importantly, stay put during breezy afternoons on the island and during boat trips.

ELECTRICITY

No doubt with all the diving gear you will wish to bring, including cameras and film recorders, there will not be much weight allowance left in your luggage for hair dryers and similar appliances. In many resorts, visitors can look quite out of place with neat blow-waved hair. On men, a shade of stubble will certainly not be frowned upon. Standard electricity supply is 220–240 volts, 40 cycles AC. Plugs are normally the round three pin variety but an adaptor is recommended as sockets vary.

Generators supply power on the islands since there is no national electricity grid. All resorts have electricity but as fuel to power the generators is expensive, many of the other inhabited islands have to make do with kerosene and candles. The inhabited islands that do have power restrict the supply in most cases to evenings – 5–11pm.

MEDICAL ADVICE

As is true for most tropical locations, vaccinations for cholera, typhoid, tetanus and polio should be considered. The only vaccination that is officially required for entry into the Maldives is yellow fever if visitors have come from a potentially infected area.

Although malaria has officially been eradicated in the Maldives, there are still a few occurrences in some of the remoter islands. The malaria virus can become resistant to certain vaccines. If you are taking a vaccine, it is a good idea to check with MASTA (the London School of Hygiene and Tropical Medicine) on the current recommended preparations. They supply the necessary equipment for repelling insects, and carrying out first-aid, including such items as mosquito nets, sterile syringes, suture packs, drip needles, alcohol swabs and sterile dressings. The 'cleans needs kit' containing the operation equipment weighs 113g (4oz) and has a Hospital for Tropical Diseases logo to clear customs. They also compile holiday/travel sheets for individuals, families and companies.

Apart from the possibility of transmitting malaria, insect bites can be very irritating. The mosquito bite causes an initial brief sting followed by an itching bump. The golden rule is not to scratch, as this causes the spot to swell, become inflamed and weep. Infection could then set in. This happened to my diving companion on one occasion. A deep ulcer formed, 2 cm in diameter, which needed a course of antibiotic tablets to clear. A commonly used method of relieving the itching sensation is to make two sharp criss-cross indentations on the swollen spot with a finger nail and then to apply a dab of saliva.

There are several ways to avoid being bitten. Mosquitoes lay their eggs on damp vegetation and earth as well as in stagnant freshwater, so avoid water-filled vessels such as tin cans. They are attracted to their prey by heat, smell and sound signals and seem to prefer hairy victims. Strong perfume and scented hair applications should be avoided.

Products containing Deet, such as Jungle Formula or Autan, help repel insects. Oil-based repellents are best as they will cover a larger area of skin before drying than some other lotions. You can also make your own Deet formula by diluting neat Deet with water (approximately 30 ml in 250 ml water) in a plastic bag then rinsing wrist-bands, head-bands, cotton socks or any other small items of exposed cotton clothing in the solution. When dried and worn, these garments will repel insects for at least 48 hours. The solution does not need to be made fresh for each application, so once made up, it can be used over and over again.

After dark, long-sleeved shirts and blouses and long trousers are the best protectors but avoid dark colours, as these also attract mosquitoes. Remember to apply repellent to exposed areas such as ankles and feet.

Mosquitoes do not like cold or draughts. Most of the resorts have ceiling fans in all rooms, as well as air conditioning. Resort staff also either spray rooms in the evenings after guests have gone to dinner or light a mosquito coil. Make sure your room is properly enclosed, with the windows secure or the mesh covering the window frames intact. If necessary, a can of knock-down insect spray is usually obtainable from reception should any insects enter the room during the day. A few resorts still use mosquito nets over the beds. If this is the case at yours, ensure that the ends are firmly tucked under and all around the mattress at nightfall before you retire and that there are no holes in the mesh.

Once every two weeks it is quite common for resort staff to fumigate the entire island. A machine, similar to a wheelbarrow in appearance and as noisy as a tractor, blasts white fumes up to a distance of 10 m. Fumigation is usually carried out when the breeze is blowing away from the main meeting areas and is completed as speedily as possible.

Travelling to the Maldives generally entails a considerable amount of time in the air and on the sea. The most effective travel sickness remedy, if taken in time, is hyoscine, also known as scopolamine, which is used in Kwells. However, it has some side-effects – a dry mouth, blurred vision and confusion. Antihistamine remedies such as Avomine, Phenergan, Framamine, Gravol and Sea Legs can also make you drowsy. For me, the best all-round remedy is Sturgeron. Moreover, sips of plain bottle water help to relieve nausea.

Stomach upsets usually occur after consuming contaminated water. If you are particularly worried about this, avoid salads and peeled fruit which may have been washed in contaminated water. Eat food that has been freshly cooked and is not highly spiced. Having said that, menus often contain curries and salads, and I have eaten plenty of both with no adverse effects. Go easy on the alcohol, which can run down the immune system, and drink plenty of bottled mineral water. Use the flask of water supplied in your room for brushing teeth and for making ice cubes if a mini-bar is provided.

A change in climate and food can often cause either constipation or diarrhoea. Should the latter occur, if no blood is passed and a high temperature is not detected, let it run its course but treat dehydration from the outset. To one litre of clean water add four heaped teaspoons of sugar plus half a teaspoon of salt, or one Dioralyte sachet and drink lots of the mixture. If you have to travel and move about, treat diarrhoea with Imodium or Arret tablets. These act fast but often have the reverse effect for a while until some form of equilibrium is established.

The main hospital is in Male and deals with routine operations. There are also a few very small hospitals on other atolls. The resorts' dive centres double as medical clinics. Hosptial facilities are often over-stretched and there may be shortages of equipment, staff and medicines.

There is a dentist in Male who provides a professional service including initial consultation. His fees are not high.

If you are planning to dive, ensure that your general travel insurance covers you adequately for diving or potentially hazardous watersports.

If you want to insure against medical and evacuation fees you can join FSAM (Flying Swiss Ambulance–Maldives (Pvt) Ltd) before departing from home. Contact:
Flying Swiss Ambulance
Postfact 259, FL-9495 Triesen, Switzerland
Tel: 075 26666

Or, in the Maldives:
Flying Swiss Ambulance–Maldives (Pvt) Ltd
Huvadhoo, Marine Drive H, Male 20-26
Tel: 324508, 324509 Telex: 77089 FSA MF
Emergency Tel: 324500 (24 hours)

There are several benefits to membership of the FSAM. It entitles you to:
- Advice from the doctor at any time during the day or night.
- An emergency call-out service – it is, however, the doctor's

decision whether the emergency warrants his visit.
• Transport within the Maldive Islands during an emergency, that is, to FSAM's clinic in Male, the Male Hospital, the decompression chamber at Club Med and Hulhule Airport.
• Free consultation and registration if you come personally to FSAM's clinic in Male. The only direct charge will be medicine and medical supplies and the decompression chamber (US$ 1,000.00 per hour if you are not covered by special diving insurance) in case of a diving accident. FSAM reserves the right to claim the costs against your insurance.
• Immediate repatriation or transfer to another hospital (Colombo, Singapore or Europe or for that matter to any part of the world) any time, day or night through FSAM's ambulance jet which is now based at Hulhule Airport. FSAM will fly anywhere in the Maldives in their amphibian Lake Renegade 250, except to Addu Atoll because of vulnerability of the open sea and the absence of radio contact while flying to and fro. They do not fly at night as it is forbidden by the Civil Aviation Authority in Male.

NOTES

DIVING

Lydia Cuthbertson under water.

Introduction
Reefs
Fish Feeding
Dive Certificates
Dive Prices
Diving Practices
Choosing an Island Base
Selected Dive Sites
Marine Hazards

BACKGROUND INFORMATION

The Maldives have become one of the world's major diving destinations. Their fame derives from the spectacular array of marine life so close to shore. Indeed many snorkellers do not feel the need to don scuba gear. Spotted eagle rays, turtles, white-tip reef sharks and a myriad of colourful fish beckon. There is a vast diversity of reef life which can be seen in a compact area. Beyond the shallows, boats will take you to favoured locations for spectacular drift diving and awesome ravines where one may encounter hammerhead and whale sharks. In shallow water mantas can be viewed as they majestically skim the crest of the reef.

Diving is a year-round sport in the Maldives although water clarity is best during the winter monsoon season, from November to March. It remains good during the rainy season, from April to October, although visibility may drop to 30m (35 yards) during stormy periods.

Lunar tides which range from 1 - 2 m (3–6ft), determine water visibility during all seasons. Incoming tides bring clear water to the atolls; outgoing tides are richer in plankton and suspended matter, lowering the visibility inside the fringing reef as well as on the outside, near channel entrances. When ocean currents meet island tidal currents the force of the water flow can be greatly increased, especially between the islands, and provides some exciting drift diving.

Water visibility is generally 50–60 m (55–65 yards), in April it can be reduced to around 25–30 m (27–35 yards) by *plankton blooms* which are a feature of the summer monsoon.

This brings strong winds from the south-west that sweep across the Indian Ocean driving the surface water ahead of them. As it flows in between the islands and away from the eastern edge of the volcanic ridge on which the Maldives sit, the wake is a fairly turbulent mixture, with deep nutrient-rich water welling up to replace surface water. Currents churning

Wind Direction

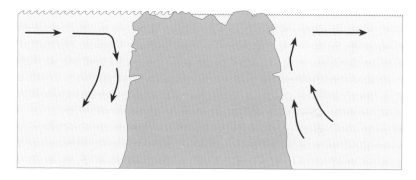

Surface Wind Upwelling

Above: Wind created 'upwelling'. Surface water is calmer on the leeward side of an atoll.

Below: Current flowing around an atoll creating mixed 'upwelled' water on the leeward side.

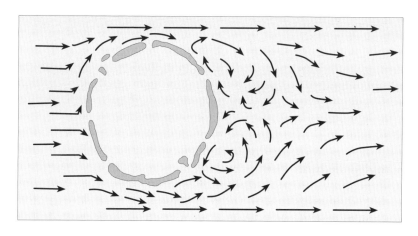

around undersea features also bring a mixture of nutrients to the surface. Upwelled water, rich in nutrients, promotes the growth of microscopic marine phytoplankton, which multiply, bloom and are in turn eaten by larger zooplankton. Such plankton blooms are generally found on the eastern sides of the atolls. What is lost in water clarity is more than compensated for by the chance to dive among whale sharks and manta rays that feed on the zooplankton. Soon after the summer months, the winter monsoon brings clearer water to most regions and the whale sharks and mantas move to western areas.

The seasons are therefore a major influence on diving in the Maldives. Weather tends to be unpredictable, with glorious sunshine followed by rain that can vary from brief, refreshing showers to day-long downpours – especially during the summer monsoon. During this time, with the wind blowing from south-west, the eastern side of the atolls will have calm surface seas, but considerable upwelling. The western side of the atolls will feel the full force of the strong winds driving the surface water before them. Seas will be choppy and some sites, especially on the outer reef, may be undiveable. The reverse occurs during the winter monsoon when fine, light north-easterly winds prevail from December to March, producing generally calmer seas and sunnier skies. The sunniest months, with the calmest seas and best underwater visibility, are usually February and March. The strongest winds and roughest seas are during June and October, and are associated with the change in wind direction. Water temperatures average between 20°C and 30°C (70-85°F) often reaching 32°C (90°F) in the lagoons.

REEFS

The underwater terrain in the Maldives affords a great number of diving opportunities. Its reefs are formed by a wide variety of corals, from low-lying rounded clumps to

North Male Atoll, approaching the east coast from the air.

Boat-building at south-west Male.

Encrusting ascidians and sponges cover rocks on a shady rock-face.

The magnificent anemone, Heteractis magnifica.

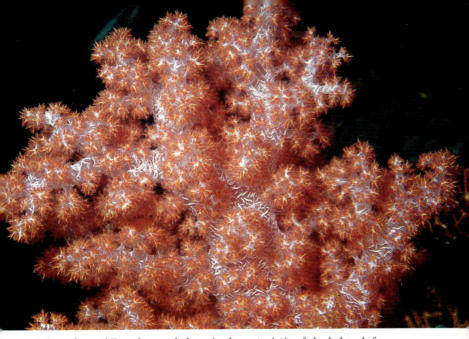

The soft coral Dendronephthya *is characteristic of shaded rock-faces.*

Gorgonians grow prolifically where there are strong currents.

The starfish, Fromia.

Opposite: This sea cucumber feeds on algal-coated surfaces.

Filter-feeding feather stars hide in crevices in the daytime and emerge at night to spread their arms into the current.

spectacular mushroom formations rising out of the sand, some well over 20 m (65ft) high, dripping with colourful soft corals. Scuba divers are rewarded with spectacular buttress-like coral formations and ravines honeycombed with caves and crevices, precipitous walls and drop-offs to thousands of metres, where diving is made easy by steady currents for drift diving.

Coral is more prolific at shallow depths, where there is plenty of light and food. As this is where most damage is done by wave action, the relatively sheltered mid-channel reefs often provide the prettiest diving with abundant staghorn, elkhorn and layered sheet coral. Large yet exquisitely formed table corals are common in the Maldives, although brain corals tend to be small in comparison to the Caribbean and Micronesia.

Throughout the Maldives the reefs are honeycombed with caves of various shapes and sizes, generally running in parallel lines. Viewed from outside, exhaling divers within fissured caves can be seen to transfer streams of tiny bubbles through apparently solid rock. The islands are criss-crossed with channels where currents are at their strongest. The walls along the deeper inner channels and some outer reefs that are not too severely lashed by ocean tides will harbour the most prolific variety of cave life. In contrast, the steep slopes and turbid water that often surround them do not create the best conditions for hard coral growth.

The profile of a reef is determined by its location on an atoll. *House reefs* can be as close to shore as 5 m (excluding the jetty which usually reaches out to the drop-off) and drop steeply, or be so far out and low-profile that they are virtually non-existent. At low tide the crest is exposed with the reef descending in a series of coral and sand steps then falling steeply to a maximum of approximately 50 m (55 yards) inside the atoll. House reefs on the lagoon side of islands perched on the outer reef will have this profile, but of course, the ocean-facing house reef will be steeper and drop to thousands of fathoms.

Channel reefs form the sides of the channels through which fast-moving currents flow. They are usually between the islands and tend to be concave and steep with overhangs, caves and caverns, levelling out on to a sandy bottom at around 35 m (115 ft). Usually the parallel wall cannot be seen but the narrower the channel, the stronger the current.

In wider channels, the relatively featureless sandy bottom is interspersed with coral humps and sub-sea hills, sometimes fragmented to form ravines and pinnacles. The crests of these mid-channel or 'tila' reefs range from 8 to 12 m (25–40 ft) with the bottoms resting at about 30 m (100 ft).

Outer reefs ring the atolls and give them their basic shape. They extend close to the sea surface and may dry-out at low tide. Sailing around the islands, it is common to see areas of flat brown coral rock surrounded by the aquamarine sea. Incoming tides crash against the outer reef. The surface coral needs to be robust to survive this constant pounding and is generally composed of brain and star coral.

Many resort islands offer interesting reef areas just a short

These turtles have been raised in a pool on Kuramathi.

distance from the shore on the fringing house reef. In some places, such as Biyadhoo, natural passages and points of entry are signposted. Many divers go night diving right off the beach in front of their own rooms.

With the increasing influx of divers, many resorts including Ihuru, Rannalhi and Nakatchafushi have designated their adjacent house reef areas of marine conservation incorporating fish-feeding programmes. This does not mean that their house reefs are any better than others. In fact, in some instances, it is because the reef was in such a poor state that the fish-feeding programme was necessary. With managed feeding life gradually takes hold again but it may not be so prolific, at least not for many years to come. For the record, Ihuru does have a good house reef and Rannalhi has a spectacular drop-off just a few metres from the beach. However, as with most diving destinations world-wide, the best diving sites and most spectacular reefs lie far enough off-shore to require access by boat. Because of the constant flow of oxygen and nutrients brought in around the atolls, the coral reefs are healthy. Marine life is flourishing and most reefs are alive with countless varieties of fish and invertebrates.

North Male Atoll was the first atoll to open for tourism with Bandos starting the famous shark-feeding station. The Kuda Bandos reserve was saved from resort development by the Government so that people could enjoy it in its natural state. It has many exceptionally good sites particularly to the south-east, but the extreme north-east and some parts of the north-west (north of the Nakatchafushi) have suffered from periodic infestation by the crown-of-thorns starfish. On the other hand, turtles nest on some islands in the north-west and resort managers have built nursery aquariums to give them a better chance of survival. Baros is one such island.

Along the north-east outer reef the coral is very low profile and extensive. Divemasters tend to keep their trips within the atoll for fear of losing divers. Even dive cruise ships tend to dive inside the outer reef here. Diving from around

Kanifinolhu south to the Vadhoo Channel is rich with excellent sites. Where currents regularly run fast, such as in channels, nutrients on which soft corals feed are brought with the stream. Here, you will see an abundant array of colours ranging from powder blue and indigo to coral pink, orange and yellow. HP Reef and Virgin Reef, referred to in the list of dive sites, offer two of the best locations for colour photography.

South Male Atoll provides much the same underwater terrain as North Male with the exception that the outer reef drops off far more steeply and to a greater depth before shelving. Large fish such as sharks and spotted eagle rays are more common here than in the north.

Ari Atoll offers truly virgin diving with plenty of opportunities to see hammerhead sharks and, in season, whale sharks.

South and North Male in particular are said to be over-dived. Boat traffic can be quite heavy during peak times – February and March – with more than one dive group at a time on a particular site. However, some resorts including Kanifinolhu set their time one hour ahead of other resorts, which means they are the first to the favoured sites and usually have them to themselves.

FISH-FEEDING

Spear-fishing and coral collection have been banned by the Maldivian government. The fishing industry is only concerned with tuna, and as they are caught away from the shallow reefs, on hook and line, the rest of the reef-fish are unmolested. Fish-feeding is very much encouraged by all dive bases. This can cause irritation to some dining-room managers, as guests raid the breakfast table in search of titbits for the fish. Some have resorted to laying just the minimum at the buffet table until the dive boat has departed.

To feed the fish, simply reserve some bread and ideally one or two hard-boiled eggs and secure them in a plastic bag in your stab jacket until you need them. The fish are very tame and used to being fed. Just a move to open the pocket of the jacket or simply a shaking of the fingers will cause interest. Six-bar wrasse can become annoyingly persistent and give nasty nips to exposed areas of skin if you are not careful. Vlaming's unicorn fish appear from nowhere in large numbers when feeding is taking place, and can be dangerous when excited. If the numbers and their ferocity become intolerable, gently put the food back into your stab jacket or discard it and gently swim away, remembering to take the empty bag back with you. Under no circumstances lash out with an arm unless it is properly protected with neoprene. Wounds are easily inflicted by the razor-sharp fins.

Some dive operators have staff who feed sharks. Some try to attract them by banging on their tanks, which is harmless but not always effective, and some place fish amongst the coral for the sharks to search out. Lion's Head is the most famous shark-feeding station (see list of dive sites). Shark-feeds also take place on the house reef of Bandos, Banana Reef near Furana, Rasfahri near Nakatchafushi and the Fish Hole in the Ari Atoll, which is accessible from Bathala, Ellaidhoo and Mayaafushi.

CERTIFICATES

To dive in the Maldives, the visitors must bring with them a medical certificate or letter from their doctor confirming their physical fitness. Dive schools are available (see A–Z resorts) for the complete novice. Qualified divers must also bring with them their certification card or any diving test certificate. Dive log books are not essential, but divemasters often ask to see them, so bring them along as well. It is also useful for repeat visitors to cross-reference dive sites, selectively building up a broad span of sites visited.

Dive operators in the Maldives normally require those divers who possess a recognised certificate but who have not logged a dive in the Maldives during the previous two weeks, to do an initial check dive with an instructor. The procedure can be tedious for advanced divers but it is a good and safe way for the first-time visitors to become familiar with new conditions and the local terrain, and it also provides a refresher for those who do not dive frequently. You will normally be charged for the check dive even if it is in a boring lagoon.

DIVE PRICES

Diving charges vary, change frequently, and are therefore difficult to keep track of. Broadly they compare to those in the Caribbean. At the time of writing, a single dive with all equipment included is US$25–30; with just tank and weights US$22–27. Six days' unlimited diving with all equipment is US$210–248; with just tank and weights US$165–230. There is a reduction for two dives a day. Dive boats are generally run by the hotel management and are therefore charged separately. It is worth checking this at the resort, as the extra cost to a dive package could be considerable – around US$18 per single boat trip and US$24 for two boat trips in one day. The dive boats usually take between 15 and 30 minutes to get to a site, although because of the location of some resorts, the journey may sometimes take around an hour depending on sea conditions. The price of the boat dive is the same regardless of distance travelled. Underwater cameras cost about US$40 for half a day and US$60 for a whole day. As with all extra items of expenditure, diving is signed for and payment made at the end of the stay. Some dive centres add an extra 5 per cent service charge, which may not be apparent until final payment is made.

Dive packages can be booked in advance from your home country, but once paid, there is no refund should you decide to cancel. However, when you are on the island, booking is more flexible – which is just as well as the weather can be unpredictable. In exceptionally poor conditions where surface visibility is hazardous the dive operator will forgo the planned boat trip and take the team of divers around the house reef.

DIVING PRACTICES

Dive schools are heavily influenced by the American PADI organisation. Multi-level diving is normal and most often done in currents. Groups are split into pairs and given a good briefing on the dive site's profile. This is sometimes done at the dive centre using sketch maps, and sometimes on the dive boat with slate and pencil.

The Maldivian government has issued several official recommendations:

Activities on board dive-boat.

- No diver should go below 30 m (100 ft).
- Decompression diving is not allowed. However, there is a recompression chamber on the island of Club Med (adjacent to Kurumba), and some further recompression capsules on various other islands including Bandos and Biyadoo.
- All divers should carry an alternative air source (i.e. an octopus rig).

Dive centre operators' opinions vary on whether these recommendations have the force of law, but most abide by them anyway.

Divers generally start the dive in a group, then disperse in the drift, diving with the current, which can be strong. Most boats operate unanchored, dropping divers off upstream then picking them up at the other end of the reef. It is important to follow the dive profile and go with the current to facilitate the pick-up. In heavy swell, when it is difficult for the boat to remain stationary, a rope will be thrown to the divers to enable them to haul themselves to the ladder. You board boat in full gear, but without your fins, which are first either handed to the boat handler or thrown on to the deck. If the boat handler decides that you need some assistance, he will hold the neck of your tank whilst you are climbing the ladder, thus taking some of the weight.

An essential diving aid is an inflatable day-glow sausage which can be inflated at a depth of 3 m (10 ft) should decompression be necessary, as there is no anchor line to hold on to and unless you are diving a familiar house reef, you may not have a reef face to hang on to. Trying to remain neutrally buoyant at the required depth for any length of time is also difficult in cross currents. The sausage is also invaluable on the surface, especially in a swell or poor weather conditions, as it is visible up to a distance of approximately 200 m (220 yards) and so aids the boat handler. Gradually more dive bases are equipping themselves with these decompression marker buoys. As a matter of course, Kurumba and Kanifinolhu issue them to all divers who do not have their own.

CHOOSING AN ISLAND BASE

North Male and *South Male* atolls cover 100 km (60 miles) of ocean from north to south. They have 10 inhabited islands and 35 resort islands, with various uninhabited islands – those which have vegetation and presumably could be, or have been, inhabited. There are also hundreds, if not thousands, of precarious tiny coral islets and sandbanks scattered around and between the islands.

The following other atolls contain resorts and therefore dive bases. Outer atolls, some of which contain inhabited islands, are not included.

Ari Atoll has 18 inhabited islands, 55 uninhabited islands and 11 resort islands. Rasdhu and Toddu are two atolls to the north of Ari. Rasdhu is inhabited, offering tourists the chance to see a Maldivian fishing village about its daily life. Rasdhu comes under the administrative umbrella of Ari.

Felidu Atoll has 5 inhabited islands, 19 uninhabited islands and 2 resorts, Alimatha and Dhiggiri. Felidu is sparsely populated, and the inhabitants eke out a living from fishing, boatbuilding and selling tee-shirts to the tourists.

Fadippolu Atoll has 4 inhabited islands, 53 uninhabited islands and 1 resort, Kuredu Island Resort. Fadippolu's inhabited islands are relatively crowded and make handicrafts from coral and mother of pearl. The atoll is a strong fishing centre. A fish processing plant was opened in 1986.

South Malosmadulu Atoll has 13 inhabited islands, 51 uninhabited islands and 1 resort island, Kunfanadu. Just south, is where Thor Heyerdahl based his book *Maldive Mystery.*

Kuramathi and Ellaidhoo (Ari), Kanifinolhu and Kurumba (North Male), Lugana Beach/Velassaru Island and Biyadhoo (South Male) and Alimatha (Felidu) are recommended resorts for divers. For anyone wanting to gain advanced diving certification up to Dive Instructor, Kanifinolhu is the place. See the A–Z of resorts for further details on dive bases and schools.

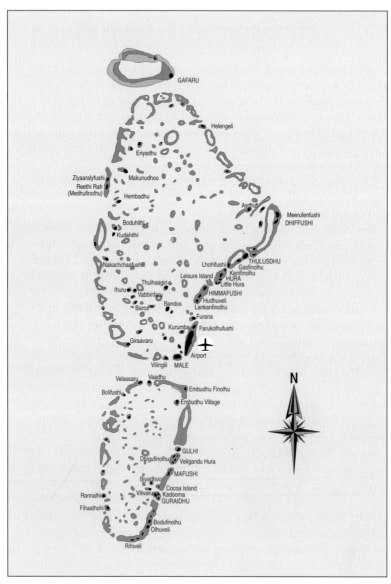

Kaafu Atoll.

Guide to the Maldives

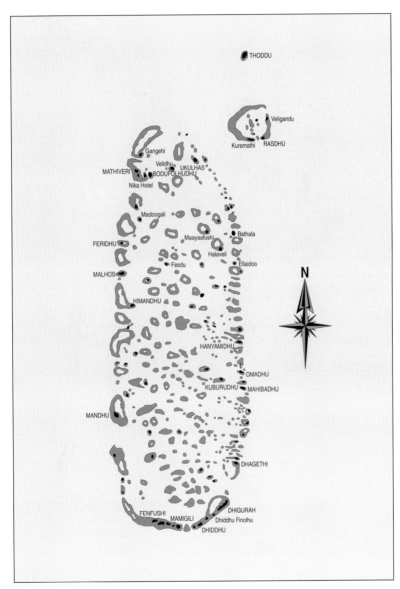

Alif (Ari) Atoll.

44   *Guide to the Maldives*

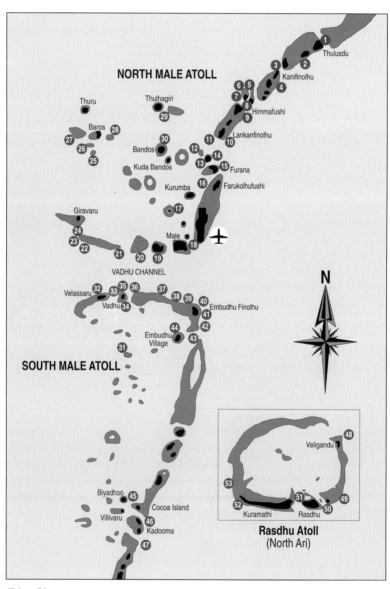

Dive Sites.

Map Ref.	Name and attractions	Depth (in metres)
1	*Thulusdu Channel* soft corals, fans, sharks	15–30+
2	*Aquarium* iridescent reef fish, corals, cave	10–30+
3	*Kani Canyon* overhangs, lobsters, groupers	15–27
4	*Kani Outside* mantas, corals, groupers, nudibranchs	15–30+
5	*Thamburudu* sea fans, nurse sharks, turtles, napoleons	20–30+
6	*Blue Lagoon* extensive hard corals, small reef fish	2–17
7	*Potato Reef* large potato cod, morays, groupers	5–25
8	*HP Reef* soft corals, napoleons, eagle rays	13–30+
9	*Devils Reef* huge sea fans, soft corals	12–30+
10	*Manta Point* mantas, whale sharks, turtles	7–30+
11	*Virgin Reef* soft corals, sharks, napoleons, turtles	10–30+
12	*Nials Reef* sharks, caves, black coral	10–30+
13	*Hannes Reef* hard and soft corals, reef fish	3–27
14	*Rowan Reef* mantas, stingrays, morays	4–20
15	*Furana Outside* whale sharks, napoleons, schools of fish	3–30+

16	*Banana Reef* sharks, stingrays, morays, reef fish	3–20
17	*Feydhu Caves* caves, overhangs, hydroids, black coral	4–27
18	*Maldive Victory* 100 m shipwreck, hydroids	10–40
19	*Villingili Caves* caves, eagle rays, tuna	5–26
20	*Kiki Reef* zigzag ledges, caves, gorgonians, napoleons	5–25
21	*Old Shark Point* sharks, eagle rays, soft corals, anemones	5–30+
22	*Lion's Head* grey sharks, tuna, eagle rays, morays	3–30+
23	*Giravaru Caves* white-tip sharks, turtles, corals, caves	3–15
24	*Giravaru Channel* mantas, whale sharks, tuna, bluefin jacks	3–30
25	*Black Coral Reef* caves, ledges, black coral, moorish idols	3–20
26	*Shallow Point* large sea mound, corals, barracuda	10–30
27	*Kukulu Faru* pinnacles of hard coral, sharks, sweetlips	15–30
28	*Baros Home Point* corals, moorish idols, leopard rays, puffer	5–25
29	*Thulagiri* barracudas, sharks, lionfish, feather stars	15–30+
30	*Shark Point* the Maldives' first shark-feeding station	5–25
31	*Echinopora Reef* table staghorn, plate corals, giant anemones	20–28

32	*Velassaru Outer* ledges, hard and soft corals, tuna	5–30+
33	*Vadhu Garden* cliffs and slopes, soft corals, reef fish	2–27
34	*Vadhu House Reef* lionfish, eagle rays, garden eels	8–15
35	*Vadhu Caves* caves, huge cavern, eagle rays, turtles	5–30+
36	*Paradise Pass* fast drift dive, sharks, eagle rays, corals	10–30+
37	*Helmut Reef* turtles, tuna, bannerfish, porcupine fish	5–20
38	*Embudhu Canyon* ravine, sharks, jacks, sponges, corals	5–30+
39	*Mystery Caves* nurse sharks, morays, soft corals, gorgonians	5–25
40	*Embudhu Caves* caves, huge cavern, morays, turtles, rays	8–30+
41	*Palisades* series of vertical walls, invertebrates	4–30
42	*Fusilier Reef* schools of fish, tuna, sailfish, marlin	3–23
43	*Embudhu Channel* fast drift dive, eagle rays, soft corals	3–30
44	*Embudhu Village North Wall* reef fish, invertebrates, octopus	2–25
45	*Biyadhoo House Reef* turtles, white-tip sharks, morays, eagle rays	5–30+
46	*Kadooma Channel* fast drift dive, sharks, triggerfish	20–30
47	*Biyadhoo Manta Point* numerous mantas, napoleons	8–30+

48	*Maddivaru* hammerhead sharks, whale sharks, napoleons	20–30+
49	*Boduga* corals, giant clams, turtles, napoleons	20–30+
50	*Rasdhu* sharks, stingrays, garden eels, lobsters	5–30+
51	*Kuramathi House* small wreck, large green moray, corals	5–25
52	*Three Palms* mantas, whitetip sharks, groupers, turtles	15–30+
53	*Fan Reef* huge sea fans, caves, lobsters, turtles	20–30+

Dive centre - Kurumba.

SELECTED DIVE SITES

Site 2 – AQUARIUM 10–30 m (33–98 ft)

Situated at the outer reef, so primarily a wall dive that culminates in a corner coral outcrop, where reef sharks can be seen circling. Good small cave full of colour – ideal for photography. As with most sites, artificial light is essential.

Large groupers, oriental sweetlips, clown trigger fish, leopard rays and mantas in season. Large grey sharks can be seen in the distance lying on the sandy bottom.

Site 5 – THAMBURUDHU 20–30 m (65–98 ft)

A drift dive through a channel with a strong current. Large sea fans jut out from the walls and various other colourful gorgonians line overhangs, Most of the dive is at 25 m. Nurse sharks are seen in small caves. Also at this site are white-tip reef sharks, turtles, green morays, emperor angelfish and napoleon wrasses.

Site 6 – BLUE LAGOON 2–17 m (7–56 ft)

Divers enter a shallow area where the white sand reflects the sun's rays which give the water a luminous aquamarine colour when seen from the surface. The soft sand gently slopes down to an oasis of exquisite hard corals at around 18 m (60 ft). It is a breath-taking wonderland of rolling valleys interspersed with table corals, plateaux of star coral, sheet coral and staghorn, all teeming with iridescent reef fish.

Site 7 – POTATO REEF 5–25 m (16–82 ft)

An excellent two-stage dive over gardens of coral. At one end of the site is a huge head of star coral. Living in the crevices of the mound are some of the friendliest eels. Due to the continual encouragement of divemasters, the eels will come out, seeking to be fed, and are not afraid to be handled. Vermilion rock cod, spotted potato groupers around 1 m (3 ft) in length, from which the reef is named, and a stingray live around this mound and will also accept food offered to them.

The reef stretches towards Girifushi then suddenly forms a large protective bowl. Sheltered in this amphitheatre is an extensive range of hard corals ranging from delicate finger growth to tall mushrooming pillars growing above layered plate corals and delicate table corals. A host of small reef fish include morays, groupers and patrolling schools of bluebar jacks.

Site 8 – HP REEF 13–30 m (43–98 ft)

One of the most spectacular dives. HP is a mound of coral-encrusted rock situated between Girifushi and Himmafushi islands. Just inside the outer reef, crystal-clear water rushes over the mound at rising tides supporting dense soft corals. The variety and beauty of the corals is astounding. As you descend around the edge of the reef from 10 to 30 m (33–98 ft), small caves and sweeping overhangs drip with pastel colours. All along the walls and beneath the ledges is a coating of living rainbow colours. Tiny brilliant blue and orange fish rise and fall over large clumps of finger coral like spray sent up by crashing waves.

Many small to medium-sized reef fish plus larger napoleon wrasses, eagle rays, bluebar and horse-eye jacks complete the scene which is set against an electric blue background.

Site 10 – MANTA POINT 7-30 m (23–98 ft)

The outer reef, seaward of Lankanfinolhu, crests at 15 m (50 ft). It is of low profile and slopes down, periodically broken by mounds of star coral to a ledge then drops steeply away to over 2000 metres. Manta's hover around cleaning stations waiting to have parasites removed from their skin and gills. They average about 4 m (13 ft) from wing tip to wing tip. Like graceful spacecraft they glide one after the other to the olive-coloured mounds where innumerable tiny luminous indigo cleaner wrasse attend their clients. Divers should approach very low, just skimming the coral rubble. Movements should be non-aggressive. Mantas appear where seasonal upwelling occurs, from June to October. Upwelled water can cause extremely strong currents. The dive group will stop at around 10 m (33 ft), cling to boulders and rocks and simply lie motionless watching the amazing spectacle overhead.

At Manta Point and a little further south on the outside reef next to Furana (Furana Outside) speckled whale sharks can also be seen as they too follow the rich upwellings.

Site 11 – VIRGIN REEF 10–30 m (33–98 ft)

Virgin Reef is an extensive sea mound situated between Furana and Lankanfinolhu islands. To one side it drops sharply forming a wall with two large coral pinnacles lying parallel to the walled side of the reef. The area has strong currents of approximately 5.5 kph (3 knots), and attracts large animals such as sharks, napoleon wrasses, turtles and mantas. Soft corals and hydroids are abundant in hues of blues, pinks, yellows and orange. The dive generally commences at the midway point and depending on the current goes either left or right.

Site 13 - HANNES REEF 3–27 m (10–89 ft)

Hannes Reef is a beautiful and easy dive; an ideal compact site in shallow water suitable for photographers. The reef begins at 3 m (10 ft) where sand and rubble slope down to a circular coral formation protruding from a sandy bottom. After traversing the mound, the divers gradually ascend, heading west along a shallow wall which provides more interest than the easterly direction. The regular direction of the current is usually mild. Along the wall are interesting small caves and coral sections. The plan should be not to rush the circular mound, as the following wall is not very long and it is inadvisable to retrace the dive against the current.

Site 14 – ROWAN REEF 4–20 m (13–66 ft)

Situated on the outer side of Chicken Island, Rowan Reef is also known as Manta Point. Large numbers of mantas can be seen here feeding and mating, especially during the winter monsoon period. Occasionally whale sharks visit this site. There are interesting caves at 20 m and shelves at shallower levels where turtles amble and rest.

Site 15 – FURANA OUTSIDE 3–30 m (10–98 ft)

Highly recommended for whale sharks, mantas and large schools of fish. Most of the dive is along the crest of the reef at 20 m (66 ft). The wall drops steeply to the left, where a look-out should be kept for the giants. Whale sharks are very tame and slow and will permit you to stroke them and, if you are lucky, to hitch a ride. Towards the end of the ridge the crest turns a corner to the right, where napoleon wrasses are seen. Then gentle sandy ledges and caves housing large lobsters provide further shallow sunny diving. At around 3 m (10 ft) there are beautiful hard corals and prolific reef fish. The backwash can be quite strong with patches of coral breaking the surface. Keep this in mind and swim to the left of the slope and deeper water for the pick-up by the dive boat.

Site 18 – MALDIVE VICTORY 10–40 m (33–131 ft)

The Maldive Victory is a 100 m (325 ft) long shipwreck lying on a sandy bottom at 40 m (131 ft). On Friday 13 February 1981 the captain of this freighter tried to taxi the ship along the runway of Hulhule Island's airport. The precise circumstances are not known but evidently he lost control and the ship sank. Positioned perfectly upright on the bed channel, the wreck is swept by strong currents. Even in the most favourable of conditions, dive boats tether lines to the ship's mast at around 10 m (33 ft). Divers then descend the lines. In heavy currents, they then proceed to climb down the ladders attached to the two masts. The deck is at about 26 m (85 ft). An anchor hangs forward over the port bow and below the stern is the enormous propeller. Divers can easily enter the wreck from the deck at the aftercastle then swim through passages to the bridge. The metal is rusty and there are many stinging hydroids, as you would expect in a regular strong current. It is, therefore, advisable to have top-to-toe protection, especially diving gloves.

Site 21 – OLD SHARK POINT 5–30 m (8–89 ft)

Situated at the corner of the deep Vadhu Channel, the reef has many anemones dotted around caves dripping with soft corals. In addition to the main attraction, sharks and leopard rays are also seen skimming the reef, like low-flying aircraft.

Site 22 – LION'S HEAD 3–30 m (10-98 ft)

This is the most famous shark-feeding station in the Maldives and is named after a gargoyle of coral shaped like a lion's head. Packs of grey reef sharks, about 2 m (7 ft) in length, patrol the point and provide the best opportunity for photographs. Dive staff arrange the divers on a rough slope of rubble and dead coral at around 12 m (39 ft), down-current. Mounds and outcrops provide natural seats but some also provide homes for moray eels. You should not be surprised to have a friendly moray eel curling around your legs.

Initially the vibrations transmitted through the water column by the approaching dive boat, followed by splash of the divers entering the water, attracts the sharks at depths of 80 m (260 ft). Sharks are inquisitive and not normally afraid of Man. The shark's lateral line is sensitive to vibrations and the combination of engine, boat and diver sounds calls them from the deep.

The shark's eyesight is adapted to dim light and they often hunt in turbid conditions or by moonlight. As soon as they see the divers they will begin to patrol just a few metres from the wall. They are also attracted to contrasting shades such as brightly coloured equipment against the subdued blue-green of the reef.

Bait is held in a secure container. As soon as the smell is released into the water, it disperses with the current. Once the shark enters the area of the smell, its feeding stimulus is instantly activated and it will swim upstream to the source. Approaching to take a fish, it swings its head quickly from side to side, lining up the offering. Small pores on the front and underside of the shark's nose sense electrical fields which stimulate the shark to bite. Exciting shots can be taken of the shark's open mouth and raised teeth just as they grab the food.

Even without bait you will see sharks at Lion's Head at around 3–5 m (10–16 ft). Sensing the vibrations of arriving divers, they will appear within a few minutes, circling close in search of food. After approximately 10 minutes these powerful yet elegant creatures will swim away and the dive can be continued along the wall with the reef face to the left shoulder, which is the normal direction of the current. Between 7 and 16 m (23–52 ft) the wall is interspersed with large clams and coral overhangs housing groupers, oriental sweetlips and napoleon wrasse. After seeing so many large sharks at one station, you may expect a bland finish along the reef. Not so. The quantity of reef fish made up of shoals and solitary species is equally rewarding.

Oriental sweetlips in foreground with a group of soldier fish.

Site 23 – GIRAVARU CAVES 3–15 m (10–49 ft)

An exciting and inexhaustible wall 10 km (6 miles) long. Descending to 10–15 m (33–49 ft), divers drift past cathedral caves and a profusion of reef fish including clown triggerfish, white-tip sharks and turtles, gradually ascending to the crest and a good variety of hard corals.

Site 27 – KUKULU 15–30 m (49–98 ft)

On the seaward side of Baros towards the outer reef, the large pinnacles of coral rise up from the sandy sea bed encircled by sharks and groups of various sweetlips.

Site 28 – BAROS HOME POINT 5–25 m (16–82 ft)

Lovely coral formations teeming with iridescent reef fish including moorish idols, puffer fish, squirrelfish, napoleon wrasses, leopard rays and sharks.

Site 29 – THULAGIRI 15–30 m (49–98 ft)

Situated in the centre of North Male Atoll, surrounded by a massive sandy lagoon and fringing reef, Thulagiri is an excellent dive for photographers. A huge hard-coral-encrusted mound rising from the bed is split by a dramatic canyon. Swift currents rush through the chasm, bringing nutrients to the soft corals and stinging hydroids along its walls. At the northern end of the canyon stands a tall pinnacle ablaze with soft corals. In addition to the colours and the spectacular terrain, there are shoals of barracuda plus numerous other fish including sharks, tuna, bluefin jacks, lionfish, angelfish and clown triggerfish. The best place for photographers to take pictures of white-tip reef sharks is to the east of the pinnacle, where they lie on a sandy area facing the current.

Site 30 – SHARK POINT 5–25 m (16–82 ft)

Just north of Bandos the reef contains an excellent variety of corals and abundant colourful reef fish including batfish and lionfish. Shark Point is an outcrop where numerous sharks and barracuda patrol. On a sandy level in mid-reef is a patch of garden eels.

Site 31 – ECHINOPORA REEF 20–28 m (66–92 ft)

Set well within the outer reef and therefore relatively sheltered, Echinopora is an excellent coral garden comprising delicately formed yet large corals with table, staghorn and plate corals in abundance. The area is like a fish nursery with many small colourful reef fish, clouds of which dart out of bush corals like sea spray. Enormous anemones with their attendant clownfish make this a photographer's paradise.

Site 33 – VADHU GARDEN 2–27 m (7–89 ft)

Just around the corner from Vadhu Caves, the reef crest suddenly stops to form a cliff of coral, the highest point barely skimming the surface of the sea and dropping to almost 30 m (98 ft). The wall is encrusted with corals and rich in marine life such as small species of shrimp, nudibranchs and delicately camouflaged scorpionfish. Progressing along the dive, the wall gradually peters out to a gentle slope of sweeping soft corals.

Site 34 – VADHU HOUSE REEF 8–15 m (26–49 ft)

This is one of the few house reefs visited by boat divers from other resorts. The reef surrounding Vadhu is extensive, the northern section being part of the Vadhu Channel wall. South-east of Vadhu, the reef is broken by a crescent-shaped sandy bed, home to garden eels. Starting at this point divers swim westward and clockwise. Running parallel to the southern reef some 40 m (45 yards) due south is a further wall, creating a wide channel and a current of over 4.5kph (2½ knots). Fish life is abundant and includes eagle rays.

Site 35 – VADHU CAVES 5–30 m (16–98 ft)

Stretching along the length of Vadhu's northern wall is a

continuous series of caverns, caves and ledges with good fan corals at the entrances to the caves. Vibrant pink, blue, and yellow soft corals abundantly line the ceilings and walls and there is a rich variety of other invertebrate life. One enormous cavern with its base at 30 m (98 ft) and ceiling at 10 m (33 ft) provides ideal multi-level diving and spectacular photographs. There are many large queen and emperor angelfish, clown triggerfish, lionfish and morays. Looking out to the deep blue Vadhu Channel, turtles, very large tuna and eagle rays can be seen cruising parallel to the reef.

Site 36 – PARADISE PASS 10–30 m (33–98 ft)

East of Vadhu is an inlet from the Vadhu Channel leading into South Male Atoll. This inlet is call Paradise Pass and has beautiful coral hills on either side. Strong currents carry divers through the Pass amidst schools of horse-eye jacks and individual eagle rays that soar effortlessly in the clear rushing water. Diving from north to south, the incoming tide will eventually carry you on to Vadhu's exceptional house reef.

Site 38 – EMBUDHU CANYON 5–30 m (16–98 ft)

At one end of this impressive ravine, a large section of overhanging coral has broken off. As the current rushes through the canyon it meets the mound of coral and rubble, creating a whirlpool of activity where white-tip reef sharks and schools of jacks surf in the wake of the fallen ledge. The sides of the walls are covered in colours, including dazzling orange sponges and yellow sea squirts.

Site 39 – MYSTERY CAVES 5–25 m (16–82 ft)

A wall drift dive starting at 20 m (66 ft), passing small caves and grottoes, and finishing at 5 m (16 ft). There are good hard and soft corals and a variety of gorgonians. The wall has an abundant variety of life including green moray eels, titan triggerfish, napoleon wrasse, nurse sharks, various sweetlips and an array of small colourful reef fish.

Site 40 – EMBUDHU CAVES 8 – 30 m (26–98 ft)

Further along, west to east, a series of dramatic caves and caverns honeycomb sheer coral-encrusted cliffs. Enormous tuna and eagle rays slice through the deep blue channel while inside the deep galleries, carved into the reef face, walls and ceilings drip with soft corals. Then a spectacular cathedral looms, about 75 m (82 yards) long and 20 m (66 ft) high, the main structure itself riddled with catacombs. The sandy floor is at 29 m (95 ft). Plastered over the entire inner surface are soft corals, low-lying sponges, diverse invertebrates and intermittent shelves staffed with dozens of cleaner shrimps.

Site 41 – PALISADES 4–30 m (13–98 ft)

Steep vertical walls teeming with iridescent life. Rainbow coloured soft corals, wispy gorgonians, anemones, sponges, countless varieties of invertebrates all creating a living and throbbing colourful veneer. The steep cliffs of Palisades break intermittently relieved by gentle slopes and huge mounds of coral providing home to large numbers of varied reef fish. Several outcrops catch the current and create mini-upwelled areas distinguishable by clouds of fish clamouring for tasty morsels carried towards them on the swirling water.

Site 42 – FUSILIER REEF 3–23 m (10–75 ft)

Fast currents running through Embudhu Channel stir plankton-rich waters around the crest of Fusilier Reef, named after the brightly coloured fusilier fish that school here to feed in vast numbers. Large yellowfin tuna and skipjacks in turn feed on the fusiliers. The chain also provides food for the sailfish and blue marlin that have also been seen along Embudhu Wall.

Site 43 – EMBUDHU CHANNEL 3–30 m (10–98 ft)

During the summer monsoon, when the wind blows from the south-west, the major ocean current flows and swirls into

South Male Atoll through Embudhu Channel. If this coincides with an incoming tide, divers are given an incredible drift dive over 2 km (1¼ miles) of fabulous reef, among huge tuna, napoleons, eagle rays and schools of iridescent fusiliers. Embudhu Channel is a throughway for schools of dolphins and divers can often hear high-pitched sounds they use to echo locate visiting divers.

Should the current not be so strong, you can slowly enjoy the beautiful soft corals near the mouth of the inlet then go on to patches of staghorn coral enshrouded with clouds of butterfly perch. A little further and a reef wall opens to expose a large cavern. Near the top of the cavern a cave branches off where huge nurse sharks can be seen lying on the floor.

Site 47 – BIYADHOO MANTA POINT 3–15 m (26–48 ft)

The dive commences by following the drift along the outer reef crest passing napoleon wrasse and schools of large tuna *en route*. The terrain is fairly scrubby. Then sweeping along and around a corner the crest rises to a sub-sea hill which peaks then drops steeply. This point is a regular manta cleaning station. The current is usually very strong. Approach low and slow then position yourself on the pyramid crest, holding on to boulders or the diver next to you. Corals and marine life are sparse. Then suddenly a few mantas appear, as apparitions at first, then more. I saw no less than seven of these giants on my first dive at this site.

Site 48 – MADDIVARU 2030 m (66–98 ft)

A truly varied and extensive site. The place for hammerhead sharks. You descend to around 20 m (66 ft) and the reef drop-off. Swimming along the crest with the reef on the right shoulder, a myriad of colour and life passes just a few inches below. The parallel channel, deep and blue, is cut by tuna and bluefin jacks and the occasional patrolling white-tip and whale sharks. Keep a keen eye out for hammerheads way-off in the deep blue. They tend to be solitary and keep well away from the reef, although on my visit a pack of seven were seen. As soon as the divemaster spots one in the deep, away from the reef, he will dart towards the shark to get a good sighting. Because of this, it is important for the team to stick close together and behave as a single body. Make about 10–15 strong quick fin kicks so as not to stray too far from the reef. Further along the crest is a spur where there is a napoleon wrasse feeding station, so if possible have a supply of hard-boiled eggs. Nearby towards the lagoon, is a snow-white sandy field at about 25 m (82 ft) where stingrays and large sharks rest on the bottom and a swaying mass of garden eels can also be seen. All around this patch is a low-lying wall encrusted with hard corals.

Schools of barracuda, 1.5 m (4 ft) grey sharks, lionfish 1.5 m (5 ft) stingrays, titan triggerfish and 1 m (3 ft) parrot fish plus countless other varieties of reef fish are all found at this one site.

MARINE HAZARDS

The primordial fear most humans have of being attacked and devoured by a terrible creature of the deep is really not justified. It is true Maldives waters are home not only to delicate, beautiful and harmless species, but also to some of the largest and perhaps most feared creatures patrolling the seas. Hammerhead sharks, barracuda, stingrays and giant whale sharks frequent certain areas. With a better understanding of their nature and motives, however, and the familiarity gained by diving amongst some of these larger species, you will soon be more confident about approaching some of the dive sites.

Sharks
Out of around 245 different species of shark worldwide, only a small minority have bitten people. The species vary enormously in their typical behaviour patterns. A calmly

swimming diver is of little interest to most sharks and is unlikely to be indentified by them as potential prey. However, if you thrash around in murky water you may confuse and attract sharks used to feeding on struggling prey. Attacks have also occurred when people have jumped into the water close to a shark, which has perceived the action as aggression. Moreover, divers can inadvertently provoke sharks by chasing and cornering them, perhaps to take a photograph, and then failing to recognise their territorial posturing. Pulling the tails of peaceful 'sleeping' sharks has also caused attack.

The sharks most likely to be encountered in the Maldives are the white-tip reef (*Triaenodon obesus*), the grey reef (*Amblyrynchus*), the black-tip (*Melanopterus*), the nurse (*Ginglymostoma*), the hammerhead (*Sphyrna zygaena*) and the whale shark (*Rhinchodon typus*). White-tip and nurse sharks will only hurt if they are cornered and teased. Whale sharks are so gentle and slow that they will actually let divers ride them. The other sharks can be aggressive, but if a shark considers you bothersome, it will generally leave the scene. However, if it lowers its nose, arches its back, points its pectoral fins sharply down and starts to swim in an exaggerated fashion, rest for a moment, then very calmly swim away.

In the very unlikely event of an attack, encourage the victim to hold the wound tightly with one or both hands if possible. Remove them from the water and rest them on the beach, in shade if possible. Continually reassure the victim. Do not remove the wetsuit. If the wound is very serious, the victim should not be moved further as this will increase the likelihood of extensive loss of blood and further shock – the main cause of death. As soon as possible control the bleeding with direct pressure using a dive glove or grain-free pebble strapped over the laceration with a dive-knife strap or weight-belt. Seek medical assistance.

Barracuda
The great barracuda *Sphyraena barracuda* varies from 1.25 to

4.25 m (4–14 ft) in length. There are about 16 species, of which the smaller ones hunt in shoals. The larger types hunt singly. Both shoaling and solitary barracuda are seen in the Maldives. The solitary barracuda is very inquisitive towards divers and will often follow them, swimming parallel, for some considerable distance. It can be quite unnerving.

Barracuda hunt by eye. They sight their prey from afar then make a lightning dash, either swallowing it whole or frantically biting pieces out of it with their razor-sharp teeth. Although they do attack humans, it usually occurs as a result of mistaken identity. A diver swimming in murky water flashing a shiny knife or a piece of jewellery can create an illusion of flashing fish scales. The risk of barracuda attack is greatly reduced in clear water.

Eels

Many species of eel are found in the Maldives. Essentially nocturnal creatures, they lie by day in coral caves or rock crevices with only the head visible. By night they use their well-developed sense of smell to hunt for sleeping fish. They will often lie coiled like a snake then strike at prey with lightening speed. Some morays (*Muraenidae*) will attack divers but usually only in defence of their home. Experienced divemasters are often able to coax the large and common green morays *(Gymnothorax)* out of their holes to feed and pet them, without feeling their needle-sharp teeth. However, this is not recommended.

The aggressiveness of morays varies from dive site to dive site. Their teeth are covered in slime which contains detritus and bacteria. The bite can be very painful, but the main cause for concern is the infection which often results if it is not properly treated. In the first instance clean the wound with freshwater or antiseptic, then immediately seek medical attention.

Poisonous Fish

Scorpionfish and lionfish (*Scorpaenidea*) and stonefish (*Synanceiidae*) have an array of poisonous spines along their backs, and the stingray has a heavily poisoned needle at the base of its tail. All these bottom-dwelling creatures are ambush predators and lie in wait motionless for prey to come within easy reach.

Stonefish and scorpionfish can barely swim, as they lack an air bladder to regulate buoyancy, and they are so confident of their camouflage that they will often let divers pick them up or just try to scuttle away if they are poked. If they do sting, however, they can inflict virtually intolerable pain and in some cases, as with the stonefish, death. Lionfish have poisonous glands in grooves along the spiny rays of the dorsal fin. They are more agile, though slow, and are not timid of divers. Although not lethal, their wounds can cause great pain.

The spines of these poisonous fish are, however, used solely as a defensive measure. They are not able to 'shoot' poison and will not attack. Therefore, to avoid an unpleasant encounter, divers should try to be neutrally buoyant and snorkellers and waders not to walk on the reef. When walking in the sandy lagoon just off the island's shore, it is advisable to wear stout rubber footwear with thick soles to avoid being stung by stingrays, and to shuffle your feet – rays will quickly move out of the way.

Injuries from poisonous fish can be treated by immersing the wound and affected limb in hot water. The protein poison is then broken down by the hot water. The duration of immersion depends on the severity of the injury. Serious wounds should be immersed for as long as possible until professional medical help is available. The Australian diver Ben Cropp says that the Aborigines chew the leaves of the *Avicennia* mangrove tree and apply the pulp to the affected area. Mangroves are quite common on many islands, so it might be worth trying.

Porcupine Fish

The porcupine fish *(Dionodon liturosus)* has not been included under the 'Poisonous fish' because, like the moray eel, it is only poisonous if eaten. However, in the course of defence, it will inflate its body with water until it is totally spherical. This

Porcupine fish - snorkelling - Baros.

action pulls out stout spines all over it's body, which is covered in a slime containing detritus and bacteria. Should you be nicked by a spine and bleed, secondary infection may set in, which could require medical attention. In the first instance the wound should be bathed with freshwater and antiseptic applied to the area. If left alone, the porcupine fish can cause no harm. They are slow-moving creatures and will try to escape by hiding in a crevice or hole. If you try to pull it out, it will inflate, locking its body in between the coral rock and making it virtually impossible to extricate. It is when inexperienced divers are persistent in trying to obtain a photograph of a blown-up porcupine that minor injuries can occur.

Sea Urchins
Urchins are very rare in the Maldives. The ones that are seen

The lined bristletooth is an abundant algal-feeder on Maldivian reefs.

The giant moray can grow to at least 220cm in length.

The blue-striped snapper is frequently seen in densely-packed shoals.

Overleaf: The bizarrely-shaped scorpion fish can change its colour according to its surroundings.

The Malabar grouper is often found in sheltered lagoons.

Guide to the Maldives

tend to be found along coral rock and ledges living side by side with lobsters. They are black with thin spines about 20–40 cm (10–15 inches) long. Occasionally small round golf-ball-sized brown urchins can be seen tightly packed into small holes in the rock, but they are difficult to make contact with accidentally.

The spines of the large type are very brittle, but they can easily penetrate a thin wet suit. Once the spines have penetrated the skin, they break off. They have tiny barbs on them, so they are virtually impossible to remove. The area will itch and cause pain. Your skin will look something like an orange peel, as the embedded spines are quite visible, like spots of black ink under the skin. Eventually they will dissolve and the wound will heal, but the pigmentation may remain for over a month.

Early treatment with hot water is very effective in relieving the pain and preventing subsequent swelling or infection. Ammonia, or urine which is a convenient substitute, can also be applied to help neutralise toxins.

Poisonous Invertebrates
Soft feathery hydroids and fire coral, which is a hydroid that secretes a stony skeleton, can be thought of as a protectors of the reef. Jellyfish and anemones also have nematocysts (stinging cells) which are strong enough to cause an itchy nettle-type rash. Contact with any of these invertebrates will cause immediate burning. The subsequent rash can last for a couple of weeks. Alcohol, vinegar or cortisone cream applied to the stung area will neutralise the poison.

The most dangerous invertebrate in the Maldives is a species of cone shell, which feeds on fish. This snail has developed such an intensely poisonous venom that it can paralyze its prey almost instantly. Treat cone shell stings as for venomous fish stings.

The prospect of a sting from a cone shell should be enough to deter you from trying to collect them. If not, the fine for doing so, which may be as high as $1000, may act as a sufficient deterrent.

Surgeon Fish

All surgeon fish have one or two pairs of scalpel-like blades situated on each side of the caudal peduncle. In defence and attack, these sharp and powerful spines are pulled out from grooves where they are normally hidden. When the surgeon fish lashes its tail vigorously, the scalpels make light work of slicing through skin and flesh, as I have found from personal experience.

Perhaps the most common and easily identifiable species are the blue surgeon fish *(Acanthurus leucosternon)* and Vlaming's unicorn fish *(Naso vlamingii)*.

The scalpel apparatus of a surgeon fish.

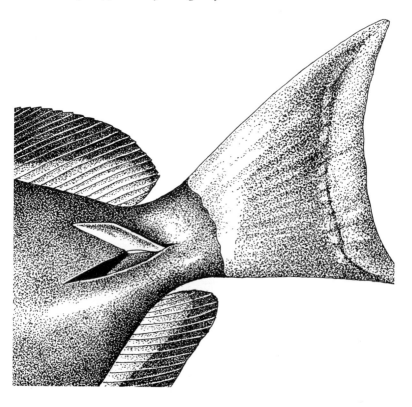

Coral Cuts
These are common injuries especially for snorkellers, with the coral being so abundant close to shore on many islands, and with the sea just barely skimming the coral heads even at high tide. Some house reefs have passages to aid the diver or snorkeller, providing easy access across the reef and to the drop-off, but coral cuts can still occur, no matter how careful you are.

If you are cut, the wound should be cleansed thoroughly with freshwater and antiseptic. If cotton wool or gauze is available, use it to scrub the wound with light up-sweeping motions to remove coral fragments and foreign particles. Seek medical attention if the cut is severe. Minor cuts heal more quickly if secured with butterfly stitches, a strong yet pliable form of Sellotape that pulls the skin together. Keep the wound dry and aerated.

Coral Ear
This is a very common infection of the ear experienced by both divers and snorkellers. It starts when the submerged victim experiences painful pressure on the ear. Seawater full of bacteria, microscopic plankton and minute detritus particles is forced down to the ear drum and surrounding walls of the ear channel. Some of the particles penetrate the delicate tissue and the bacteria infect the ear. Pain can be excruciating, especially several hours later, making it difficult to sleep at night.

To avoid coral ear, remember to equalise *before* you descend and continue equalising until you are neutrally buoyant or in the case of snorkellers positively buoyant. As soon as you feel any pain, ascend a metre or so until it subsides then continue the dive if you want to. Once infected, the ear will remain delicate and susceptible to future occurrences. After the infection there can be slight deafness, which can last for a year or more.

After each dive, thoroughly rinse your ear with freshwater. Try and take a small bottle in your dive bag whenever you dive and rinse soon after surfacing. If you leave it until you are back at your room, salt crystals will have formed in your ear, making it more difficult to cleanse it thoroughly.

Once pain has set in, a few drops of olive oil, readily available from the dining room, gives quick relief lasting several hours. In severe cases, some dive centres will provide antibiotic ear drops but as you can imagine, these supplies are extremely valuable in a place so remote and where hundreds of visitors learn to dive each year and many suffer from coral ear.

Your family doctor can prescribe ear drops that come in two complementary preparations. The first loosens particles and cleanses the ear, while the second dries the ear. I find the latter produces irritating crystals which I eventually have to rinse out with water anyway.

The best way to ensure your safety and enjoyment is to know and respect the environment you are in. Divers should be neutrally buoyant on the reef and snorkellers should swim and not crawl over it. Coral should not be collected alive or dead. People who are careless or aggressive and cause damage to the environment may well be stung, stabbed or bitten by creatures which are only trying to defend themselves.

RESORTS

Pool at Laguna Beach resort.

Introduction
A-Z Resorts

INTRODUCTION

An A–Z of Maldives resorts follows but it is worth remembering that the beautiful islands are not generally noted for their cuisine. However, the quality and variety of food and accommodation is constantly being improved and tailored to meet guests' tastes. Remember too that during the high season – January, February and March – the islands can be fully booked and crowded.

Several resorts including Kanifinolhu, Kuramathi, Bandos, Baros and Kurumba have recently been upgraded. One of the major complaints in all resorts, second only to the plain food, has been the salty bore-water showers. Virtually all of the resorts used to pump water from the ground, then filter it through sand. Occasionally it was heated, which caused it to emit a pungent sulphuric odour, but generally it was left unheated. In very hot and humid weather, tepid showers are refreshing but after a heavy downpour the unheated water becomes very cold. After a dive it is good to have a hot freshwater shower. Unheated saline water is difficult to wash in as ordinary soap will not lather, so if you have a salty shower, use hair and body shampoo instead. Using a body moisturiser helps to avoid tacky-feeling skin.

About two thirds of the resorts now have desalinisation plants, and others collect rain-water in barrels. Do not use this water to drink or brush teeth. Flasks are provided in the rooms which are constantly topped up with freshwater to drink and use for ice-cubes if a mini-bar is available.

Some resorts offer a child-minding service with baby cots available on request. Special-occasion cakes can also be arranged by contacting the housekeeping division.

All bills are signed for at the resort, and the final account settled before departure, with a 10 per cent service charged on all bills from the restaurant, bar, coffee shop, general shop and laundry service.

The service of the resort staff on most islands is warm,

efficient and courteous. To show your appreciation, a small tip may be offered in rufiya or US dollars. It is also advisable to have rufiya if you are visiting fishing villages or island-hopping and intend to do some shopping. Currency may be exchanged at the resort reception, where current rates are displayed at the counter.

Standard recreations are diving, snorkelling, windsurfing, *dhoni* sailing, day and night fishing, volleyball, badminton, tennis, table tennis, videos, cultural shows such as the national *bodu beru* dances, island-hopping – including shopping trips to Male – board games and libraries. Even at resorts where the clientele is international, the books in the library tend to be German. Stocks depend on donations from guests. English editions are snapped up quickly, so bring plenty with you.

Some islands also have swimming pools and some have football pitches where guests can compete against resort staff.

Most resorts advertise parasailing and water skiing but there are few speed boats around the islands. They are costly to repair, so most are maintained only during the high season when the sea is calm and favourable for these sports. The main recreation, throughout the year, is diving, with motorised *dhonis* being used as dive boats. So if you want to parasail or water ski, you are less likely to be disappointed if you visit the Maldives during the high season. Special arrangements can usually be made to get a speed boat from another island should one not be available at your resort at any time during the year, but this would of course increase the cost of a session dramatically.

A-Z RESORTS

Alimatha Aquatic Resort
Felidhoo (Vaavu) Atoll
Tel: 350544
Fax: 350575

Airport: 61 km (38 miles)

70 modern bungalows with unheated saline showers, 17 with air conditioning.

This Italian-run medium-range resort includes excellent Italian food in its menu. Because of its close proximity, visit nearby Dhiggiri via Club Vacanze.
 The resort is close to the outstanding Vattaru reefs and also has a decompression chamber – something not common in the Maldives. Sailing, catamarans and canoeing are available plus free windsurfing.

Angaga
Ari Atoll
Tel: 350510
Fax: As above
Telex: 66155 ANGAGA MF

Airport: 106 km (66 miles)

50 individual air-conditioned bungalows, all with hot and cold freshwater showers in open-air Maldivian-concept bathrooms.

Angaga is a new resort nestling in the middle of South Ari Atoll, a fair distance from the outer reefs. Divers are unlikely to see hammerheads or whale sharks in these relatively sheltered internal waters but they will be compensated with a great variety of corals and reef life not able to withstand the constant battering of the ocean waves.
 After just a few years in operation, this resort has had time

to 'settle' and mature to the demands of the discerning visitor. Ari resorts tend to be higher in price than many of those in the North and South Male Atolls, the main reason being the greater distance to ferry construction and maintenance materials and provisions. The resort has a bright and airy feel and the guest rooms are well appointed and decorated to a high standard. The Dolphin Bar extends out on to the beach where sun loungers on the sand provide a pleasant vantage point to view the setting sun. The lively can dance to the strains of 'bodu beru' drums on Maldivian entertainment nights.

Angaga has tall palms and masses of soft white sand and yet snorkelling and shore diving are excellent. The house reef is only 5–7 m (16–23 ft) from the beach! A pathway shaded by shrubs and palms provides an easy stroll around the island within 20 minutes. With just 50 bungalows, the island does not feel crowded. Each of the bungalows has a private sandy veranda with an *undhoalhi* (swing) hanging from the ceiling, and leads straight out on to its own section of private beach.

Angaga owns an adjacent island about 20 minutes boat ride away, where a very good coral reef beckons divers and snorkellers.

The dive operation is run by Angaga Prodivers. A full range of courses is offered from the Resort course and Open Water Diver to Assistant Instructor. Divemaster and Assistant Instructor courses take three weeks each and include a minimum of 25 dives. One month's advance booking via fax or telex is required for Rescue, Divemaster and Assistant Instructor courses. Medical records not older than one month are also required. A certificate for CPR training is required for the Rescue course. At the time of writing, the Open Water Diver course at Angaga costs US$346 and the Assistant Instructor course, US$690. Diving equipment, school material and boat trips are included in these prices

Angaga Pro Surfers offer certificate courses in surfing and sailing. Water skiing and parasailing facilities are also available.

Ari Beach Resort (Dhidhufinolhu)
Ari Atoll
Tel: 350513
Fax: 350512

Airport: 97 km (60 miles)

76 rooms of which 45 are air-conditioned bungalows and 14 de luxe suites. Fresh hot and cold showers.

Ari Beach has a full range of facilities and activities including windsurfing, catamarans, sailing, fishing, canoeing, tennis court, football, water skiing, parasailing, island-hopping and excursions to Male.

The house reef is close to the shore, offering excellent snorkelling and diving. This is one of the islands favoured by Hummingbird Helicopters as an excursion destination; it is also close to several inhabited and uninhabited islands should you wish to island-hop.

Asdu Sun Island
North Male Atoll
Tel: 345054
Fax: 345051

Airport: 37 km (23 miles)

30 bungalows with unheated freshwater showers. No air conditioning.

Asdu is situated to the north-east of Male Atoll near Meerufenfushi, and is the head of a sand spit several miles long. Because of the extensive sandy lagoon, shore diving is not recommended. Activities include windsurfing, fishing, canoeing, water skiing and island-hopping, including shopping trips to Male. Remember, however, that *dhonis* travel at approximately 13 kph, so a *dhoni* trip to Male could prove to be quite an exhausting morning if the sea is choppy.

Athurugau Island
Ari Atoll
Tel: 350518
Fax: 350508

Airport: 68 km (42 miles)

38 air-conditioned bungalows with hot and cold freshwater showers.

Athurugau has a mainly Italian clientele and a good reputation for food. It has a big sandy lagoon on one side of the island and corals close to the shore on the other. It is close to some very good dive sites in the atoll and is also close enough to the outer reef for deep drift diving and the chance to see large pelagics. Activities include catamarans, fishing, canoeing and island-hopping.

Avi Island Resort (Velidu)
Ari Atoll
Tel: 350595
Fax: As above

Airport: 64 km (40 miles)

50 bungalows with unheated freshwater showers. No air conditioning.

Situated amidst some first-class dive sites in the North Ari Atoll, it also has a good and easily accessible house reef. Activities include windsurfing, fishing, canoeing, tennis and football.

Bandos Island Resort
North Male Atoll
Tel: 343310/342527/343876
Fax: 343877

Airport: 8 km (5 miles)

205 rooms of which 90 have air conditioning, including some de luxe suites. The rooms are built in single-storey terraces along the beach and encircling the island, with hot and cold freshwater showers.

This large resort has recently been upgraded and is still growing, with an emphasis on local style and more character. There is a 24-hour coffee shop offering an a la carte menu, an interesting Sand Bar on the beach and an air-conditioned restaurant. A beachside disco and further oriental restaurant is planned. Kuda Bandos, a nearby uninhabited island, has been made into a public reserve.

Bandos is a busy divers' resort with a well-equipped watersports centre, Dive Bandos. Comprehensive courses for both diving and windsurfing are offered. Bandos is said to be the diving capital of the Maldives and used to be the base for Voightmann's 'shark circus'. This is where divers first started to feed the sharks mouth to mouth.

The island is almost circular, with a very narrow and shallow lagoon surrounding it. Snorkelling is exceptional over the edge of the reef which is 20–30 m (22–35 yards) from the narrow beach. Although the distance to the drop-off is short, it can prove difficult to get across the reef crest at low tide. However, the dive centre posts the times of high and low tides on a board each morning and provides a trolley (not usually available on the islands) for shore divers to transport heavy gear around. The great advantage of Bandos is that shore diving is possible all around the island. Because of the difficulty of crossing the reef, an underwater path has been made by the dive centre, which leads to the reef edge where the wreck of a yacht can be found at the bottom of the drop. The dive centre is the most popular point of entry but there is another channel by the main jetty. There are three dive boats that carry first-aid kits, oxygen equipment and ship-to-shore radio. In an emergency, the boat will radio the dive centre and head for the main chamber at Club Med. The dive centre radios Club Med to warn them, and Club Med despatches a speedboat to intercept the *dhoni* and complete the journey.

Approximately 25 dive sites are visited on a regular basis but as Bandos is near three other resorts (Kurumba, Farukolufushi and Furana) some sites are often shared, which can mean considerable traffic. Hot and cold drinks are planned for the dive boats plus 'sausage' marker buoys. Night diving is arranged every day for experienced divers around the house reef.

There is a classroom for CMAS and PADI dive tuition to Advanced certification, a darkroom with an E6 processing and projection facility and video-editing desk, plus film sales and a proper equipment store. A full range of Nikonos products is available for hire, and also a Sony Handycam video camera in a housing. Divers are advised to bring film and tapes (Video 8).

There is a decompression chamber, two flood lit tennis courts and a grill restaurant. Activities include windsurfing, catamarans, sailing, fishing, tennis, football, water skiing, island-hopping and shopping trips to Male. The general consensus of opinion among visitors to Bandos, however, is that the island is not particularly attractive, and it is somewhat lacking in atmosphere. Perhaps this is due to the large number of rooms in a relatively small area.

Baros Holiday Resort
North Male Atoll
Tel: 342672
Fax: 343497

Airport: 16 km (10 miles)

50 bungalows, of which 20 have air conditioning. All the rooms have unheated freshwater showers.

Baros is a small, very pretty half-moon-shaped island with a good lagoon on one side for windsurfing and an excellent small house reef on the other side for snorkelling. Most of the rooms are situated on the reef side of the island. Popular with British visitors, this resort is one of the oldest, having opened in 1973.

Sub Aqua Reisen of Munich runs the diving school and offers all grades of certification up to CMAS 3-Star and all PADI courses up to Divemaster. Theory classes are held in the coffee shop, and practicals take place in the shallow bay leading to the reef edge. Sea and Sea 35 mm cameras are available for hire but you should bring your own film, as this is in short supply and quite expensive. The dive boats carry VHF radio and first-aid-kits but no portable oxygen, although there is a large oxygen set at the dive base.

There is one access point to the house reef for shore divers just beyond the bay where open water tuition takes place. Scuba tanks ordered in advance will be left on the beach in the shade next to the drop-off, which is about 30 m (35 yards) from the shore. Divers then pick them up when they need them during the day and just a couple of steps takes them into the water. At the end of the dive, the empty cylinders are left on the beach where they will be collected by the dive centre's staff. This saves a lot of effort lugging tanks and full dive gear across the island.

Snorkellers can enjoy corals just a few yards from the beach, where the drop-off is about 10 m (33 ft) away in some areas. This is definitely the place to fall out of bed and slip straight into the beautiful warm sea for an early-morning snorkel! A forest of stag horn coral teeming with coloured fish is just 2 m (6 ft) from shore. The rooms are positioned towards the west – perfect for topping up the sun tan in the warm late afternoon.

Activities include windsurfing, sailing, fishing, water skiing, island-hopping and shopping trips to Male.

The *al fresco* Turtle Restaurant has a sandy floor and is named after the young turtles reared in the small pool next to it.

Bathala Island Resort
Ari Atoll
Tel: 350504
Fax: As above

Airport: 58 km (36 miles)

36 small round thatched bungalows with air-conditioning. The garden showers provide unheated saline water.

This very small and compact friendly island is Maldivian in style and is a sister resort to nearby Maayaafushi. Popular with German visitors, it is peaceful and quiet, the main attraction being the excellent diving. Bathala offers shark-feeding, drift diving and exciting shore diving. The house reef is just 30 m (33 yards) from the beach, with a drop-off to 45 m (50 yards). The diving is run by a German, Robert Schmidt. The windsurfing is free but as the currents can be very strong, surfers should be experienced. Sailing, fishing and water skiing are offered.

Biyadhoo
South Male Atoll
Tel: 343516/343978
Fax: 343742

Airport: 29 km (18 miles)

96 air-conditioned rooms in six strips of two-storey colonial buildings overlooking the beach and gardens. Hot and cold freshwater showers.

This 10 hectare (25 acre) resort run by the Taj Group is an ideal size, large enough to walk around and explore, yet small enough not to feel too rambling. The beaches are very pretty with snorkelling and shore diving a dream. The restaurant nestles in the lush interior surrounded by tall palms. Full windows enclosing the restaurant create an open aspect. With air conditioning, first-class service and excellent food, this is one of my favourite resorts. The bar/coffee shop adjacent to the restaurant is beautifully situated and well stocked. A large patio provides a cool area to sit by the bar and is also used for al fresco dining on barbecue evenings. It's fascinating watching the fruit bats (flying foxes) overhead at dusk.

Fresh vegetables are occasionally supplied by the hydroponic garden in the centre of the island. All around the island grow an assortment of tropical fruits. During the summer monsoon – April–October – coconuts fall frequently. First comes the sound of an almighty *'crack'*, shortly followed by a loud thud. Try to keep to the paths where staff have usually dislodged any loose coconuts by shaking the trees or throwing missiles at them.

The Nautico Watersports Centre runs the diving on both Biyadhoo and its adjacent sister island, Villvaru. It is quite a small centre and can become crowded with divers at meeting times, but the diving is exceptional from both boat and shore. PADI Open Water Certification is available. Because of the time factor and the numbers of divers they have to cater for, the divemasters are not keen to provide any advanced or specialised courses unless large numbers are involved. The theory is done in the open-air thatch-roofed lounge next to the dive centre and practicals in the beautiful small sandy lagoon just in front of the centre. PADI manuals are in extremely short supply – students are usually just given photocopied pages to study from. If you plan to learn to dive anywhere in the Maldives, it might be a good idea to purchase your manual at home beforehand, even though the price of the course should include the manual and the certification card.

International Windsurfing Association courses are also available for beginners and intermediates. Practice for this also takes place in the lagoon.

Divers should not miss a trip to Manta Point. On the one occasion I dived this site, after an arduous battle against the current to the steep raised coral outcrop, my group witnessed no less than nine mantas hovering around the point feeding.

Biyadhoo house reef has excellent sites around the island with entry passages signposted. Passage 1 is the most diverse.

Follow it to the drop-off then swim right. The corals and fish life are beautiful and abundant including numerous anemones, clams, morays, turtles, eagle rays, white-tip reef sharks, groupers and many more. Then a spur from the wall shoots out to the left into deeper water. At this corner is a large coral mound with small caves and a resident shoal of oriental sweetlips. Just to the right of the head is a beautiful high table coral ideal for photography. Further around the reef is a valley of delicate hard corals. The house reef is so good and close to the shore, that it's tempting to forego boat dives. Of particular interest are the green turtles *Chelonia mydas*, regularly seen here and in several other areas of the Maldives. The Nautico Watersports Centre is efficient, with a well-equipped medical hut. It also has a Drager decompression pod.

On the island there is a clearing in the tall palms where regular football matches are held between guests and staff on the large tarred pitch at around 5 pm. Volleyball is also played on an adjacent court. If the heat and humidity are too much for you, you are always more than welcome to watch – make sure you lather on the mosquito repellent though. There is a convenient beach bar/coffee shop a couple of yards away. Sailing and fishing trips are also available. A free ferry service operates between Biyadhoo and Villivaru for those wanting a change of scenery.

Boduhithi Coral Isle
North Male Atoll
Tel: 343198/343981/342573
Fax: 342634

Airport: 29 km (18 miles)

88 character cottages, air conditioned, with unheated freshwater showers.

This very pretty and popular resort mainly caters for Italians. Visits can be made to nearby Kudahithi. Free windsurfing, catamarans, sailing, canoeing and water skiing are available.

Bolifushi Island Resort
South Male Atoll
Tel: 343517
Fax: 345924

Airport: 14 km (9 miles)

32 chalets, including 16 air-conditioned over-water wooden cabanas.

Bolifushi offers dving, windsurfing and water skiing, but a less than average range of sports facilities.

Farukolhufushi (Club Med – also known as Faru)
North Male Atoll
Tel: 344552/343749/343021
Fax: 342415

Airport: 3 km (2 miles)

152 rooms including 19 two-storey blocks with air conditioning, all with showers, providing fresh water most of the day.

This island is instantly recognisable by its enormous sweeping thatched Swahili-style roofs. Day-trips or single-night stays are not permitted, as the addition of 'floating' visitors to the watersports-inclusive packages offered could cause administrative problems.

Faru is close to many popular dive sites which are also frequented by other resorts; it is also close to Male for shopping trips. A photo lab is available to those who can't wait to have their shots of sharks developed.

It has an interesting beach and many activities during the day such as gymnastics, aerobics, yoga, volleyball and underwater slide and video shows. Catamarans and windsurfing are available, plus football, but no water skiing or tennis.

Cocoa Island (Maakunufushi)
South Male Atoll
Tel: 343713
Telex: 77037 COCOA MF

Airport: 40 km (25 miles)

8 rooms built in two-storey units. No air conditioning. Unheated saline showers.

Cocoa Island is a very high-quality resort offering good food and wine. Being so small, it is often competely booked up by one group. So exclusive is it that day-trippers are not permitted.
   The beach is good and watersports include windsurfing, catamarans, fishing, water skiing and parasailing.

Dhiggiri Resort
Felidhoo (Vaavu) Atoll
Tel: 350592
Fax: As above

Airport: 60 km (37 miles)

30 rooms including 3 with air conditioning. Unheated freshwater showers.

This resort has fewer that average recreational facilities, but free windsurfing is offered. Sailing is available and diving is excellent, offering generally virgin terrain.

Dhigufinolhu Resort
South Male Atoll
Tel: 343599/343611/343734
Fax: 343886

Airport: 19 km (12 miles)

50 air-conditioned bungalows, many with open-air toilets. Showers are unheated and saline.

This is a small and lively resort which has recently been renovated to a very high standard and attracts a mainly German clientele. Between this island and neighbouring Veligandu is a deserted island reserved exclusively for the Veligandu and Dhigufinolhu guests.

Windsurfing is available, plus catamarans, sailing, fishing, canoeing, island-hopping and excursions to Male. *Dhonis* take snorkellers to the reef.

Ellaidhoo
Ari Atoll
Tel: 350614
Fax: As above

Airport: 58 km (36 miles)

36 cottages including 3 with air conditioning. Unheated saline showers. The accommodation also includes some interesting wooden huts on stilts over the water.

This is an Italian-run resort, run by the same people as Boduhithi and Kudahithi. There is excellent diving at nearby sites. Do not miss a trip to the famous Fish Hole. Recreational facilities include free windsurfing. Sailing is also available although snorkelling is not recommended.

Embudhu Finolhu Island Resort
South Male Atoll
Tel: 344451
Fax: 345925

Airport: 8 km (5 miles)

40 rooms, of which 24 are air-conditioned water bungalows. The remainder do not have air conditioning and are situated on the beach. Hot and cold freshwater showers.

Embudhu Finolhu is a new Australian-run resort. It is a very small, narrow sandy island with no natural shade or house reef close by. However, diving is available and excellent as the island sits on top of the cusp of Vadhu Channel and the greater outer reef. Snorkelling gear is available but there is not much to see in the vast sandy lagoon. It is an island for windsurfers and there is also a tennis court, catamarans, water skiing and island-hopping trips.

Embudhu Village
South Male Atoll
Tel: 344776
Fax: 342673

Airport: 8 km (5 miles)

98 chalet bungalows, some with air conditioning. Hot and cold freshwater showers.

This larger than average resort is much bigger than Embudhu Finolhu. It is popular with the Germans. It has a good professional dive centre, an excellent house reef and snorkelling close to the good beach. Many other dive bases drop divers off at the mouth of Embudhu Channel for a drift dive leading to the house reef of Embudhu Village. Windsurfing, water skiing, fishing, island-hopping and Male excursions are available.

Eriyadu Island Resort
North Male Atoll
Tel: 344487
Fax: 345926

Airport: 39 km (24 miles)

46 bungalows, mostly built in terraced sections close to the water's edge. No air conditioning. Unheated freshwater showers.

This is a large resort surrounded by a wide beach and plenty of natural shade. It has a beautiful lagoon and a good house reef. The diving is with Swiss Sub-Aqua. Plenty of island-hopping excursions are available including shopping trips to Male. Water sports include windsurfing, catamaran sailing and water skiing.

Fesdu Fun Island
Ari Atoll
Tel: 350541
Fax: 350547

Airport: 64 km (40 miles)

50 round thatched cottages. No air conditioning. Unheated saline showers.

Fesdu is a bright, fresh, lively island in the increasingly popular Ari Atoll. It has a good house reef for snorkellers and divers; boat diving is excellent.

The beach is good for sunbathers and an interesting sand bar runs down to the lovely lagoon. For those wanting to get further away from it all there is a small deserted island close by just for Fesdu guests.

Fihalhohi Tourist Resort
South Male Atoll
Tel: 350541
Fax: 350547

Airport: 45 km (28 miles)

76 air-conditioned rooms, including one de luxe suite. Unheated freshwater showers.

This is a big island which still has natural jungle in the interior. Subex Dive Centre provides instruction in English, German, French and Spanish. The house reef stretches long and wide providing good snorkelling and shore diving. The island has a large windsurfing school. Catamarans, sailing, football, water skiing and island-hopping are available.

Fun Island Resort (Bodufinolhu)
South Male Atoll
Tel: 344558/343597
Fax: 343958

Airport: 39 km (24 miles)

88 rooms of a high standard with air conditioning and hot and cold freshwater showers. Several of the rooms are built in terraced strips. All have their own patio just a few paces from the beautiful beach.

This minute island, 30 m by 800 m (35 yards by 875 yards) at its furthest points, can feel a little overcrowded with the large number of rooms. However, it has recently been upgraded to a high quality and very upmarket resort and has the benefit of two even smaller deserted islands nearby which can be walked to at low tide for total escapism – but be careful not to get marooned.

The lagoon is breath-taking, shallow and sandy, perfect for swimming or just lolling around. A terrace bar constructed of dark wood extends over the lagoon with plenty of space and comfortable seats where you can sip a cooling drink and watch beautiful fish in the clear water by day and the romantic sunset in the evening. For the lively, there is also a disco.

The well-organised diving school, Delphis Dive Centre, is Dutch owned and run. Although qualifications are accepted, an initial dive check is carried out on the house reef. This is one of the few resorts that offers BSAC courses. PADI courses are also available up to Assistant Instructor level. Several Sea and Sea and Nikonos III cameras and an underwater Video 8 camcorder are available to divers but you should bring your own film as stocks can be limited.

The dive centre uses about 30 sites, none more than 30 minutes away by *dhoni*. The boats have first-aid equipment, oxygen and radio and if necessary they can use Club Med's decompression chamber, which is 30 minutes by speed boat from Bodufinolhu.

Snorkelling is not very interesting in the sandy lagoon, but the island does have a jetty which extends to the edge of the house reef and provides easy access to the best snorkelling site. Shore divers and night divers also use this access point, where Reef Sharks and various rays are often seen. Night dives by boat are organised at least once a week, more often if there are sufficient numbers.

Day trips can be made to Embodufinolhu; they include lunch and dive trip to the Vadu Channel famous for fast drift diving.

Other watersports available are windsurfing, water skiing, parasailing, catamaran sailing and deep-sea fishing. If it is edible, your catch is cooked for you on your return.

Furana
North Male Atoll

At the time of writing, Furana is closed for renovation, but it is worth a few words on what it was like before its closure. Just 3 km (2 miles) from the airport, it is close to the capital for shopping trips and it is also on the doorstep of the most popular dive sites in North Male Atoll. It previously had 88 rooms, including air-conditioned terraced units and 10 luxury suites. It was Australian owned and was popular with families, particularly because of its proximity to the airport – useful for families on long-haul flights making a short stop-over break.

Gangehi Resort
Ari Atoll
Tel: 350505
Fax: 350506

Airport: 71 km (44 miles)

25 rooms, of which 8 are over-water bungalows. No air conditioning in any of the rooms. Showers are unheated freshwater.

Although there is no air conditioning, Gangehi is a fairly exclusive resort in the North Ari Atoll offering excellent dive sites.

Facilities include windsurfing, catamaran sailing, *dhoni* sailing, fishing, canoeing, island-hopping and excursions to Male.

Gasfinolhu Resort (Tree on a Sandbank)
North Male Atoll
Tel: 342078
Fax: 345941

Airport: 18 km (11 miles)

30 cabanas. No air conditioning. Unheated saline showers.

Gasfinolhu is a very small island and exclusive resort. Sports and recreational facilities are very limited although diving and windsurfing are available, plus sailing and canoeing.

Giravaru Resort
North Male Atoll
Tel: 344203/343880/343881
Fax: 344018

Airport: 11 km (7 miles)

48 air-conditioned bungalows built in terraces and two-storey blocks including some de luxe suites. All rooms have hot and cold freshwater showers.

Recently revamped, Giravaru is a neat upmarket resort with a freshwater swimming pool. The island is small – it takes just 15 minutes to walk around it – and has fine beaches, although not much natural shade. The lagoon is large for windsurfing and water skiing. In addition to having a good house reef, Giravaru is situated on the edge of the deep Vadhu Channel which offers some of the best diving in the Maldives.

The island has a large lagoon for windsurfing, water skiing and catamaran sailing. There is also a tennis court.

Halaveli Tourist Resort
Ari Atoll
Tel: 350559
Fax: 350564

Airport: 84 km (52 miles)

30 thatch-roofed bungalows. No air conditioning. Unheated saline showers.

This small Italian-run resort is just 700 m (750 yards) in diameter. It is surrounded by a dazzling white beach and a fabulous lagoon. There is free windsurfing and windsurfing trips can be arranged to nearby Bathala and Maayafushi. PADI diving courses are available. Catamaran sailing and water skiing are also offered.

The sand-floored restaurant specialises in a wide variety of pasta dishes and Italian food.

Helengeli Tourist Village
North Male Atoll
Tel: 344615
Fax: As above

Airport: 52 km (32 miles)

30 bungalows, including 14 suites. No air conditioning. Unheated saline showers.

Situated towards the tip of North Male Atoll, Helengeli is a small- to medium-sized resort. The good house reef is close to shore offering snorkelling and easy diving. However, all along this north-eastern stretch of outer reef the terrain is low-profile and extensive. Current can be strong and it is easy for divers to get lost because of the bland terrain. Divemasters therefore tend to keep dive excursions to the inside of the atoll, which provides limited scope for the advanced diver.

Helengeli has a freshwater swimming pool and offers windsurfing, fishing, island-hopping and Male excursion trips.

Hembadhu Resort
North Male Atoll
Tel: 343884
Fax: 328344 (Male office)

Airport: 39 km (24 miles)

44 bungalows, just a few with air conditioning. Unheated saline showers.

The island has a good beach and is close to the outer reef for better than average diving. Facilities include windsurfing, sailing, fishing, water skiing and island-hopping.

Hudhuveli Beach Resort
North Male Atoll
Tel: 343396/343982/343983
Fax: 343849

Airport: 14 km (9 miles)

44 rooms either in single-storey terraced units or individual thatched rondavels built along the centre of the island. No air conditioning. Unheated freshwater showers.

Under the same management as Bandos, this is one of the smallest resort islands – 750 m by 45 m (800 yards by 50 yards). Being so small, there are government restrictions on further building. It is surrounded by a huge shallow lagoon, approximately 7 m (23 ft) deep. A boat takes snorkellers out to the house reef each morning and afternoon. There are good windsurfing facilities and as the lagoon is very big, it is ideal for beginners. Catamarans, sailing, fishing, water skiing and island-hopping trips are available.

Because of the sandy lagoon, diving is done by boat and the journey to the dive sites takes between 10 minutes and an hour. Most of the dive sites used by Hudhuveli are to the south of the island and to the edge of the atoll. These same sites are usd by other islands such as Kurumba and Bandos. Night dives by boat are arranged according to demand.

The dive centre, which is owned by the Hudhuveli resort itself, is presently being refurbished and offers NAUI (National Association of Underwater Instructors) qualifications from Beginner to Open Water 1 levels. There is a Sea and Sea 35 mm camera for hire. The dive boat carries first-aid equipment and oxygen.

Activities include windsurfing, catamarans, fishing, water skiing and island-hopping. Arrangements can also be made to visit a local fishing village on nearby Himmafushi.

There is an interesting fish farm here with sharks, rays and turtles. The dining room and open-air coffee shop are attractive and the sand-floored reception doubles as the bar.

Ihuru Tourist Resort
North Male Atoll
Tel: 343502
Fax: 345833

Airport: 16 km (10 miles)

40 thatched bungalows with hot and cold freshwater showers. No air conditioning.

Ihuru is an island that many visitors have fallen in love with. Australian managed, it has been much photographed; a beautiful tiny island with shady palms encircled by a fabulous house reef close to shore. The rooms are on the water's edge. The restaurant offers a varied menu and there is a refreshing over-water bar.

The Swiss-run diving school, with a high ratio of instructors to students, offers excellent diving. Not to be missed is the very good house reef, known as the Wall. A fish-feeding programme has been in operation for some years and guests are encouraged to feed the myriad fish life around the shores. As on many islands, a favourite pastime for guests is an after-dinner stroll along the jetty with a piece of bread to feed the fish along the way. Crabs will also line up on the sand in the hope of a morsel. Early mornings and evenings are the best times for fish-feeding and this is when larger fish such as baby reef sharks and sting rays are commonly seen very close to shore.

Sailing is available, and the windsurfing is free.

Kandooma Tourist Resort
South Male Atoll
Tel: 344452
Fax: 345946

Airport: 27 km (17 miles)

52 rooms in either detached bungalows or single-storey terraced units. Rooms in the terrace do not have air conditioning, but the 20 bungalows do. Unheated freshwater showers.

Opened in 1985, Kandooma is a large island with a lake in the centre. There is no house reef to speak of but the beaches although small are beautiful and unspoilt. The lagoon is not as clear as at some other resorts.

There is plenty of organised activity including windsurfing, and football. Visits to a nearby inhabited island, Guaraidhoo, can also be arranged.

Kanifinolhu Resort (often referred to as Kani)
North Male Atoll
Tel: 343152
Fax: 344859

Airport: 19 km (12 miles)

113 rooms, from basic to 47 de luxe air conditioned cabanas with hot and cold freshwater showers. The de luxe ones are well worth the extra cost.

Kani is a long moon-shaped island about 750 m (800 yards) in length and 180 m (195 yards) wide. It is surrounded by a shallow lagoon. The house reef is not close to the shore, but it is fairly easy to swim to from the jetty in calm water and provides excellent diving. A forest of tall pinnacles of coral, some 5 m (16 ft) high with sandy-bottomed passages creates some very interesting and unusual terrain.

The dive centre is first class – certainly one of the very best in the Maldives. Run by Eurodivers, it is conveniently based at the end of the jetty, and all diving gear is securely stored in individually numbered baskets. All diving facilities are provided, including a tank of freshwater for rinsing gear. Preparation for a dive is effortless, you only have to carry your gear a couple of yards from the store to the boat. The centre is well equipped, clean and very well run. On top of all this precision organisation, the staff are friendly and create a pleasant and relaxed atmosphere.

Recognised qualifications are accepted, but any diver who does not have a dive logged in the previous two weeks is required to make a check dive with one of the instructors in the lagoon. This is useful for the first-time visitor, as it is an ideal opportunity to locate the house reef, which is about 20 m (22 yards) across an expanse of featureless sandy bottom.

A full range of PADI courses is available up to Assistant Instructor. The compressor is also situated at the dive centre at the end of the jetty, which means that the sound of the motors is not heard from the guests' patios or the beach.

Sea and Sea and Hanimex 35 mm amphibious cameras are available for hire, and also Aladin dive computers. All snorkel equipment is provided free of charge (which usually means that there is not much demand) but a motorised *dhoni*, which is also free, takes guests to the house reef each day in the mornings and afternoons. The journey takes about 10 minutes. The beaches all around the island are very good. However, on the widest lagoon side, where the jetty is situated, there is a large amount of sea grass which swirls in the water and is deposited on the shore, and it is therefore not very pleasant to swim in. There is a section of lagoon where windsurfing lessons take place that has been cleared of the grass. From above, one can see the sharp long line on the lagoon floor where clear sand meets grass.

Snorkelling from the beach is rather uninteresting, apart from the northern end of the island, where the deep channel between Kanifininolhu and Lohifushi sweeps around a corner; a fair amount of marine life can be seen here. Just a little further along the beach, a walk out across the very shallow lagoon, picking your way through coral rubble and some interesting mounds, will bring you to the reef edge. Here a wide variety of small and large fish can be seen along the reef top and down in the channel. The distance from this edge to the shore is about 150 m (165 yards). Fairly high, strong waves crash at this reef edge when the tide comes in, making it unsuitable for snorkelling.

Boat dives visit some excellent sites including caves where nurse sharks are regularly seen. Twenty-three sites are used, varying from 10 minutes' to 1½ hours' journey away. Some of the sites are used by other divers but as Kani's time is one hour ahead of that of most other resorts, the dive boat can get to them before anyone else. The afternoons are also more leisurely, as the boat can depart an hour later. Inflatable decompression marker buoys are automatically provided for use on the surface when conditions are rough or in heavy rainfall. Night dives are organised on demand and are made on the house reef, which is reached from the jetty.

Dive package costs are high but the all-round standard and quality of tuition is exceptional.

The restaurant provides limited fare, with buffets twice a week in the evenings. Most visitors, however, seemed reasonably content with the frequent curried meals. Moreover, if you order well in advance, a special meal will be prepared for you. The dining room, although basic, has character with rattan blinds which are unfurled to protect guests in wet or windy weather. Large round tables are shared.

A wide main path runs in front of most of the rooms, which means that there is little privacy on the patios.

There is a free floodlit tennis court, an al fresco bar with a sand floor, a very attractive coffee shop and bar which extends to the water, offering fabulous views across an aquamarine lagoon and Lohifushi in the distance. Here, in the evenings, rays and eels swim close to the terrace bar, creating added interest.

Free windsurfing is available. Other activities include catamarans, sailing, fishing, parasailing, island-hopping and Male excursions. Slide and underwater video shows are given during the afternoons if the weather is bad, and also in the evenings. One of the dive instructors will give a running commentary, which is usually in German first as there tend to be more Germans than English-speaking visitors.

Kudahithi
North Male Atoll
Tel: 344613
Fax: As above

Airport: 29 km (18 miles)

6 individually designed cottage suites, named Sheik's Room (which has a huge bath), the King, the Rehendi (Queen), Captain's Cabin, Safari Lodge and Maldivian Apartment. All have air conditioning and hot and cold freshwater showers.

Kudahithi is a small, luxurious resort. One of the most exclusive islands, it is ideal for those seeking solitude in comfort and style. Each cottage has its own private power boat for zipping across to Boduhithi just a couple of minutes away. *Dhonies* ferry Kudahithi guests to Boduhithi for diving and evening recreation. There is no night-life on Kudahithi but during the day water skiing, parasailing, tennis, dingy sailing and free windsurfing are available. There is also a football pitch.

Kunfanadhu
South Malosmadulu (BAA) Atoll

At time of writing, there is no information on this resort. Throughout the islands, resorts are continually being closed for renovation. Moreover, some inhabited islands are made into resorts, while some resorts are converted to accommodate islanders. Kunfanadhu appears to be in limbo at the moment.

Kuramathi
Rasdu Atoll, North Ari
Tel: 350556/350525
Fax: 355327

Airport: 58 km (36 miles)

202 rooms in three separate resorts. The most exclulsive is Blue Lagoon Club, with a mainly German clientele. The next is Cottage Club and is used mainly by Italians and Japanese. Finally there is Kuramathi Village, which is mixed but predominantly British. All have hot and cold freshwater showers. Blue Lagoon Club has air conditioning.

Kuramathi Village is the best location if you want to do a lot of shore diving and snorkelling. Blue Lagoon Club and Cottage Club are best situated for windsurfing.

Kuramathi became a resort in 1970. It is 1½ km (1 mile) long and 550 m (600 yards) across at its widest point, and is the largest resort island in the Maldives.

It has an excellent and very interesting house reef just 30 m (35 yards) from the main jetty at Kuramathi Village, where a small sunken boat is home to a large green moray eel called Big Emma. A little further along the reef, the *Reindeer*, sailing from Mauritius, was wrecked here in 1868.

Kuramathi Village is a mixture of terraced units and individual thatched rondavels. A tangle of shrubs and trees in their natural jungle state stretches from the Village to Cottage Club, where pretty whitewashed rondavels are set in gorgeous colourful gardens containing abundant bougainvillea, hibiscus and jasmine.

Further along the island is Blue Lagoon Club. Here, 20 air-conditioned cabanas are built over the water. Private steps lead down to the luminous aquamarine lagoon providing immediate access for bathers. Sitting on the wooden terrace, one can feed the fish which are clearly visible just a few feet below. With one small piece of bread, the water explodes with frenzied action as shoals of silver fish compete. A further 30 air-conditioned rooms are situated on the other side of the island about 30 m (35 yards) away where the glorious beach and lush vegetation provide small alcoves for sun-worshippers. The beach rooms have additional open-air showers at the back to rinse off seawater and sand before entering the rooms.

Beyond Blue Lagoon the island's natural jungle extends to a small powder-white sand beach and a further sandbank which stretches for approximately 3 km (2 miles) where one can stroll in beautiful surroundings. Be sure to keep an eye on the tide and be sufficientyly protected from the sun. Just inland from this point an ultra-exclusive villa is nearing completion, designed to accommodate a large family or private group.

Diving is operated by Inter Aqua Diving and is the home base of the *Sea Explorer*. Dive cruises are organised regularly on demand. Each complex has a dive centre and windsurfing base, restaurant, bar, shops and amusements such as table tennis and board games. During the low season (April–October) Cottage Club is much quieter than the other two resorts, and the dive centre closes. It takes about 1½ hours to walk around the island. Some islands in the Maldives have hard-packed paths or intermittent concrete slabs, but Kuramathi's are generally quite soft under foot. If you want to dive the house reef regularly and are based at Blue Lagoon, the walk will take about 25 minutes at a steady pace. There is secure storage at Kuramathi Village, but if, like me, you like to take your camera, video equipement, mask and fins back to your room, it can be quite an arduous journey in the extreme heat and humidity. Arrangements can be made at the dive centre at Blue Lagoon for a boat to take you to Kuramathi Village, but its usually easier to just amble down when you want. The diving is very well organised, with friendly and efficient staff. The best dive site in the area, approximately 15 minutes away by boat, is Maddivaru, where several hammerhead sharks and the occasional whale shark have been seen.

The windsurfing facilities and tuition are excellent. Water skiing, parasailing and *dhoni* sailing are also available, plus visits to the adjacent inhabited island of Rasdu, a fishing village where you can see Maldivian people about their daily life. Deserted islands are also close by for island-hoppers. Guests can eat at any of the three resorts, although many tend to stay in their own area. Full-sized tennis courts are available.

The food and service is very good on Kuramathi and although it is a very large island, it is pretty with varied scenery. I am told that one of the reasons why the plants do so well is that the sandy soil is regularly mixed with cow dung, specially shipped from India.

Kuredu Island Resort
Lhaviyani Atoll
Tel: 330337
Fax: As above

Airport: 129 km (80 miles)

170 bungalows with unheated freshwater showers.

Established in 1976, Kuredu is the most remote of the resorts and was originally just a base for divers. It has since been enlarged and upgraded and is now very popular for big-game fishing.

Facilities include windsurfing, catamarans, fishing, water skiing, island-hopping and Male excursions. There is also a football pitch.

Kurumba Village
North Male Atoll
Tel: 342324/343081/343084
Fax: 343885

Airport: 3 km (2 miles)

158 rooms ranging from twin-bedded units to suites and family rooms with interconnecting doors. All the rooms have air conditioning and hot and cold freshwater showers and baths. The bathrooms are luxurious, with good tiling and fixtures including hair dryers.

Kurumba was built in 1972 and underwent extensive renovations in 1987. All the accommodation is classed as de luxe and set in beautifully maintained gardens with a prolific bougainvillea avenue cascading rich colours on to the main path leading to the restaurants. The island is very smart and colourful with numerous healthy plants. The large freshwater swimming pool is a joy to behold, with water flowing out of terracotta urns as a central feature. Good sun loungers are plentiful.

There is regular live entertainment, and a chic and spacious cocktail lounge with adjacent bar. First-class cuisine is offered in a choice of spacious character restaurants – Chinese, Indian, Oriental and International – as well as a barbecue terrace/beach grill and a delightfully fresh French-style coffee shop which also serves very good food. Guests on full board who have daily set menus will find their choice limited and bland. However, the breakfast buffet is there for all to enjoy and includes anything from a full English-style breakfast to enormous urns of home-made yogurt.

Kurumba has a convention hall with full facilities, three floodlit tennis courts and a sports complex including table tennis. Windsurfing, catamarans, fishing, football, water skiing, parasailing, island-hopping and Male excursions are offered.

The dive centre is another Eurodivers base and offers all the PADI courses to Dive Master level plus some speciality courses: Underwater Photography and Marine Biology. Sea and Sea Motormarine 35 mm and Nikonos V cameras with a choice of lenses are available for hire, plus Aladin Pro dive computers. The island stocks film and batteries but they are expensive so it is a good idea to bring your own supply.

Kurumba uses the decompression chamber at Club Med across the water, 20 minutes by *dhoni*. All divers are required to have an alternative air source. Those without will be loaned an octopus rig, usually free of charge. Decompression marker buoys (day-glow sausages) are handed to divers who do not have their own. First-aid equipment and oxygen are carried on the dive boats.

The house reef surrounding the island comes fairly close to the beach in many places and provides easy access for snorkellers. Corals are healthy and the fish life abundant, but as Kurumba is so close to many excellent dive sites, it is perhaps a good idea to take advantage of the central base and explore. Snorkelling can be done at any time during the day.

About 20 sites are used regularly covering the south-east corner of the North Male Atoll and the Vadhu Channel. The furthest site is about 50 minutes by *dhoni*. The divemaster is excellent at briefing all the divers on the boat prior to dives and uses a large slate to sketch the site's terrrain and dive plan. Dive gear can be left on the boat in between dives during the day. Large crates are provided for overnight lock-up on the jetty. The resort management do not allow night dives.

This is one place in the Maldives where you can go for sophistication and fine food and wines. Kurumba has it all. It is much more than the publicised 'stop-over' island, although compared to the other islands it does have a faster-moving pace with a quicker turn-around of clients. The staff remain though, and they provide excellent and friendly service.

Laguna Beach Resort (Velassaru Island)
South Male Atoll
Tel: 343042
Fax: 343041

Airport: 11 km (7 miles)

58 air-conditioned rooms with hot and cold desalinated showers/baths. Standard rooms, which are of high quality and well appointed, are in two-storey units of four each close to reception and the main meeting areas, with individual bungalows of equally high standard in quieter settings. There is also a two-storey unit of four suites.

Velassaru, perched on the edge of the Vadhu Channel, has been a resort island for many years. It is ideally situated for divers wishing to see the many sharks that regularly frequent the Lion's Head site near Giravaru and the many exciting caves and canyons in the Vadhu Channel's walls.

Extensive rebuilding was carried out during 1990, the island was renamed to include the prefix Laguna Beach Resort. All around, everything appears brandnew and spotlessly clean. The many plants are very young, apart from palms and some large shrubs which have been retained from the original island vegetation. An interesting waterfall with giant clams creating breakwaters has been erected in front of the reception area. There is an ornamental pool with a Japanese-style bridge, a good swimming pool with a swim-up bar, a children's pool and a large open-air jacuzzi which is popular. Ideal for families, Laguna also offers a baby sitting service.

Unusual for the Maldives, Laguna has a choice of restaurants: Summerfields, which serves set-menu meals for half-board and full-board guests; the Café Laguna, which serves salads, light meals and snacks; the Four Seasons, a Western restaurant, serving continental cuisine; the Dragon Inn, a Chinese restaurant specialising in Schezuan and Cantonese specialities; and the Palm Grill, situated on the beach and serving quality cuts of meat and succulent sea food. The Triton Bar by the pool is split-levelled and has a lively disco and band most nights.

The rooms offer split-level accommodation with music, hair-dryers in the bathrooms and universal adaptor plugs, and are situated around the circumference of the island. The centre houses the resort staff and is the hub of the resort management.

The beaches are beautiful and spacious all around the island. Just a few hundred yards from the north shore, the reef drops sharply into the Vadhu Channel and countless fathoms swept by strong ocean currents. Unfortunately, because of the unpredictability of these currents, snorkelling is not recommended beyond the reef crest. The rest of the island is surrounded by a vast spectacular sandy lagoon, ideal for windsurfing and swimming but very limited for snorkellers. As there is no house reef to speak of, diving is by boat.

Divecentre Laguna is owned and run by a German, Herbert Unger. This small dive centre is situated in the middle of the main jetty. It has no lock-up storage, although rinsing facilities are available. Gear must therefore be taken back to your room. However, divers who wish to do a morning and afternoon dive on the same day, can leave their full gear on board the boat.

There are three instructors offering either an Introductory Resort course or a PADI Open Water course, but no advanced or speciality courses. Aladin dive computers are available for hire. Underwater camera hire is planned for the future. Dayglow decompression marker buoys are issued to all divers at no extra cost.

A no-limit diving programme can be booked only by very experienced divers. It is a package for six days' continuous diving. You have to prove that you are capable of diving independently and at your own risk. You must present an Advanced Open Water licence or CMAS 2-Star brevet or something equivalent and a log book with at least 30 dives. The last dive should have been within the last 18 months.

Laguna is around 40 minutes by *dhoni* from Male and many of the boat dives are a good 30–40 minutes away. The dive centre will not take their boat diagonally acorss the channel to the popular *Maldive Victory* wreck, because of the strong currents and heavy swell. The dive boat, although apparently sound and seaworthy, is spartan with narrow slatted seats and minimal protection against storms. The iron ladder has narrow 2.5 cm (1 inch) rungs, which are hard on the feet when you are climbing aboard with full dive gear including weights and tank. When drift diving, the boat is constantly on the move so you have to be quick to grab the ladder and climb on board. It is not uncommon for a rope to be thrown to straggling divers in choppy waters during the summer monsoon period.

Inter Aqua Surf & Sailing School, a member of VAW (The United Wind-Surfing Training Association) offers extensive windsurfing courses and certification. Boards are ACS (Air Compact System) and F2s (Fun and Function). Sailing courses are also available and catamarans can be hired for the 3–4 hour trip to Bolifushi.

Ferries run frequently to Male for shopping or sightseeing.

Island-hopping and night fishing trips are offered, plus snorkelling trips to the Vadhu and Bolifushi house reefs. Parasailing and glass-bottomed boat trips are also available.

Lankanfinolhu Tourist Resort
North Male Atoll

At the time of writing Lankanfinolhu is closed for renovation.

Leisure Island (or Kanuhura – also known as Tari)
North Male Atoll
Tel: 342881/343950/343850
Fax: 344650

Airport: 16 km (10 miles)

24 air-conditioned rooms in two terraced buildings. Unheated freshwater showers.

Leisure Island does not have a beach or lagoon but the resort tries to compensate by providing intimacy, quality restaurants and a disco. It is mostly visited by Italians. Facilities include windsurfing, catamarans and sailing.

Little Hura Club
North Male Atoll
Tel: 345934
Fax: 344231

Airport: 16 km (10 miles)

43 cottages built across the centre of the island with a choice of two modest beaches. 18 cottages have air conditioning and there are two air-conditioned de luxe suites. Unheated freshwater showers.

This compact resort has a 'solid' feel. There are few palms and little natural shade. You can walk across to the adjacent island of Hura, which has a mosque built by the Huraa dynasty of sultans in 1759. Windsurfing and sailing are available.

Lhohifushi Tourist Resort
North Male Atoll
Tel: 343451
Fax: As above

Airport: 18 km (11 miles)

60 cabanas, a few with air conditioning, including some suites. Unheated saline showers.

Lhohifushi is situated on the roaring edge of the atoll separated from Kanifinolhu by a deep channel. At the corner of this channel there is good shore diving, but the rest of the house reef is sandy and relatively featureless.

The dive centre is owned and run by Manta, a Swiss travel company that have two other dive centres in the Maldives. PADI courses offered are Open Water, Advanced Open Water, Divemaster and Rescue Diver. The theory is taught under the palms, and practicals are held in the shallow lagoon. Night dives are made on the house reef at the corner of the channel.

Twenty-seven dive sites are visited regularly, ranging from Meerufenfushi at the north-east edge of the atoll to the Maldive Victory wreck between Male and the island of Hullule. One-, two- and six-day safaris are offered. Six-day safaris visit the Ari Atoll. The dive boats have first-aid equipment, oxygen and VHF radio.

A Nikonos IVA camera with flash is available for hire plus hand lamps and dive computers. You should bring your own film.

There is a football pitch on the island and windsurfing is also offered. Although the island is not as pretty as some others, it is in a good location for visiting many dive sites.

Mayaafushi Tourist Resort
Ari Atoll
Tel: 350529
Fax: As above

Airport: 61 km (38 miles)

60 thatched rooms in units of 4. No air conditioning. Unheated saline showers.

Mayaafushi was recently renovated and is aimed at the younger market (up to the mid-thirties). Singles will feel quite comfortable, as there is plenty of action with beach barbecues, picnics on uninhabited Magala and discos.
   A house reef is accessible on the eastern side of the island for good diving and a fabulous lagoon stretches for miles to the west. The outer reef is just 30 minutes beyond and is frequented by the marine giants – whale sharks.
   Mayaafushi is a regular point of call for various dive cruises. There is free windsurfing and catamaran sailing. Water skiing and fishing excursions are also available.

Madoogali Resort
Ari Atoll
Tel: 350581
Fax: 350554

Airport: 79 km (49 miles)

35 de luxe bungalows with air conditioning and hot and cold freshwater showers.

This is a very upmarket resort, set amidst some excellent dive sites and close to the outer reef for deep drift diving.

Makunudhoo Club
North Male Atoll
Tel: 343064/345092/345093
Fax: 345089

Airport: 35 km (22 miles)

31 palm-thatched bungalows with unheated freshwater showers. No air conditioning.

The island, which opened for tourism in 1983, is large with good beaches. It has a 25 km (15 mile) reef close by with many wrecks. Because of this, and the good anchorage, it is popular with passing dive cruises and pleasure yachts. There are also plenty of yachts for charter moored in the lagoon.

Facilities include windsurfing, catamarans, sailing, fishing and water skiing. Island-hopping and Male excursion trips are also arranged.

Mirihi Island Resort
Ari Atoll
Tel: 350501
Fax: 350500

Airport: 116 km (72 miles)

26 rooms with air conditioning and hot and cold freshwater showers. Beach bungalows have thatched roofs. Over-water bungalows are of the wooden cabana style.

Mirihi is a lovely fresh new resort. The clientele is mainly Austrian, German and Swiss. The accommodation and cuisine are of a high standard and facilities include a whirlpool. The island has masses of beautiful soft white sand and the lagoon is huge. Because of this, snorkellers may find the underwater scenery limited. However, boat trips to dive sites nearby will certainly prove exciting.

Windsurfing, catamarans, water skiing and fishing trips are available.

Moofushi Resort
Ari Atoll
Tel: 350517
Fax: 350509

Airport: 89 km (55 miles)

45 air-conditioned bungalows with hot and cold saline showers.

This is another new resort in the Ari Atoll, with a mainly Italian clientele and a good range of water sports and recreational facilities. Moofushi is situated on the outer reef, thus offering a greater chance of seeing the large pelagic fish. It has corals close to shore on one side of the island whilst the other side offers a sandy lagoon. All along the west coast of the Ari Atoll sea conditions can be rough during the summer monsoon when the south-westerly winds blow. Dive boats will still venture out in quite poor conditions but will not travel too far. Snorkelling may not be viable either. Inside the atoll and to the east during this time, conditions are fairly calm.

Windsurfing, sailing, fishing, canoeing, water skiing and island-hopping are available.

Nakatchafushi Tourist Resort
North Male Atoll
Tel: 343846/343847/342665
Fax: 342665

Airport: 23 km (14 miles)

51 thatched rondavels with air conditioning and fresh hot and cold showers/baths, 26 of them de luxe suites.

This small pretty island has a very big lagoon, with a depth of around 13 m (43 ft), and is ideal for windsurfing. It also provides interest for snorkellers in places. To the south of the island, the reef edge is close to the shore, and therefore provides good snorkelling but shore divers may be disappointed because of the damage caused by the crown of thorns starfish. In addition to snorkelling off the beach, the hotel also provides a boat to take snorkellers to nearby reefs.

Nakatchafushi has beautiful beaches and a long sandspit on the western end of the island which is much photographed.

The International Dive Centre Nakatchafushi is run and owned by a German company. Although diving qualifications are accepted, the first dive is always a check dive carried out on the house reef. PADI courses are available up to the level of Advanced Open Water and CMAS up to 2-Star Diver. Underwater cameras are available for snorkelling only. Underwater torches can also be hired. Between dives, equipment can be hung on racks to dry by the dive centre but there is no secure storage and equipment is left there at your own risk.

Nakatchafushi uses around 15 dive sites regularly, the furthest being 40 minutes away by *dhoni*. The crown of thorns starfish has caused extensive damage to the west side of the atoll, most of it to the north of Nakatchafushi. However, the good sites the centre uses are further south towards the edge of the spectacular Vadhu Channel and still not too far away. Night dives can be made on the house reef. Boat night dives can also be arranged but if they are, it is usually at the expense of one of the two day dives. Full-day dive excursions are sometimes arranged to the Ari Atoll, subject to demand.

There is a very attractive terrace bar over the water. Activities available include windsurfing, catamarans, sailing, fishing, water skiing, parasailing, island-hopping and Male excursions.

Nika Hotel (Kudafolhudhoo)
Ari Atoll
Tel: 350516
Fax: 350577

Airport: 68 km (42 miles)

16 luxurious bungalows with beautiful shower rooms in a garden setting. Hot and cold freshwater. No air conditioning. Mosquito nets hang over the huge beds.

Nika is a very high-quality resort, and is said to be the most expensive in the Maldives. The island is surrounded by jetties where one can park a yacht or drop off directly on to the house reef to do some snorkelling or diving.

Italians designed the resort and manage it. The restaurant, where all meals are taken, serves a wide range of Maldivian and Italian food, delightful seafood and hearty steaks. Barbecues are held twice a week and there is an extensive variety of Italian wines. Nika has a bar, a coffee shop and a night club, also free unlimited tennis on a flood-lit court, volleyball, badminton and free windsurfing. Fishing excursions are arranged. Snorkelling is excellent and there is very good diving in the area.

There is a deserted island close by where guests can be dropped off for an afternoon and have total privacy to play Robinson Crusoe or whatever fantasy comes to mind. It is said that the island is offered first to honeymooners.

Olhuveli Club
South Male Atoll
Tel: 342788
Fax: 345941

Airport: 35 km (22 miles)

50 rooms with unheated saline showers. No air conditioning.

Olhuveli is planning renovations to its resort. However, it is considered to offer good value and good food. At low tide, guests can walk or swim to an adjoining island. Although good for windsurfing, the surrounding waters do not provide good snorkelling or diving close to shore. A boat takes snorkellers to the nearest reef. Swimming is not advised at all on one side of the island as the current is very strong and unpredictable.

The dive centre is run by Eurodivers and uses some excellent sites in the vicinity, particularly in the Gurudhu Channel.

There is an attractive bar and restaurant. Activities include sailing, fishing, catamarans and water skiing.

Rannalhi Tourist Village
South Male Atoll
Tel: 342688
Fax: As above

Airport: 37 km (23 miles)

50 thatch-roofed bungalows, 6 with air conditioning and hot water. The remainder have unheated showers. All water is fresh for approximately five hours a day.

This resort is pretty, with soft white sands, yet more wild-looking than some others. Like Biyadhoo, it has extremely tall palms in the interior (listen and watch out for falling coconuts!). The resort is Maldivian in style with good beaches and the coral drop-off is just 10 m (11 yards) from the beach. Rannalhi's dive centre is continually working on its marine sanctuary for corals and fish, which provides much to see for divers and snorkellers alike. The rooms are situated at the other end of the island at the main centre and the beach. There is an attractive over-water bar and an a la carte restaurant and coffee shop.

The dive centre is well stocked and managed but the best local dive sites are more than an hour away by *dhoni*.

Reethi Rah (also known as Medhufinolhu)
North Male Atoll
Tel: 342077
Telex: 77046 RERARE

50 bungalows with unheated freshwater showers. The bungalows are built in units of four, motel style.

This Swiss-managed resort has masses of fabulous beach and a glorious shallow lagoon for windsurfing and water skiing. It is a very flat island with few palms but ample tall shrubs to provide natural shade. The restaurant offers very good food and the coffee shop, which serves drinks and snacks, is beautifully located over the clear blue water of the lagoon.

The dive base is run by Eurodivers and also offers catamaran sailing. The Mistral School of Windsurfers provides tuition from Beginner to Intermediate certification.

Because of the extensive lagoon, the house reef is a very long way out (approximately 150 m (165 yards).

Rihiveli Beach Resort
South Male Atoll
Tel: 343731
Fax: 344775

Airport: 40 km (25 miles)

46 thatched rondavels. No air conditioning. Unheated showers which are occasionally freshwater.

Rihiveli is a high-quality French-managed resort. Situated on a massive sandbank, it is surrounded by acres of shallow sandy lagoon. Just a few hundred metres away in the same lagoon are two uninhabited picturesque islands called Rising Sun Island and Island of Birds. Guests can wade to them comfortably at low tide. The main jetty, where arrivals are deposited, is 25 m (27 yards) long.

This resort offers al fresco dining and a high standard of cuisine, and is favoured by romantic couples and honeymooners.

Eurodivers run the dive school but because of the limited house reef, shore diving is not recommended. There is a range of PADI courses on offer. Many free watersports include windsurfing, catamarans, snorkelling equipment and dinghies. There is also a saltwater swimming pool and a tennis court.

Thudufushi Island Resort
Ari Atoll
Tel: 350583
Fax: 350515

Airport: 69 km (43 miles)

42 bungalows including some de luxe suites. No air conditioning. Hot and cold saline showers.

This new resort has a beautiful large lagoon on one side and a house reef close to the shore on the other. Although fairly close to the outer reef, Thudufushi is inside the atoll and is not, therefore, subjected to much wave battering in the summer monsoon period.
   Windsurfing, cat-sailing and canoeing are available.

Thulhagiri Island Resort
North Male Atoll
Tel: 342816
Fax: 342876

Airport: 11 km (7 miles)

30 air-conditioned bungalows with hot and cold saline showers, including some de luxe suites.

After refurbishment, Thulhagiri was reopened to visitors at the beginning of 1991. Operated by Club Med, it is much smaller than its sister resort Faru and would appeal to Club Med's quieter and perhaps more discerning clientele. It is popular with French and Italians.
   Diving is available but unfortunately the crown of thorns starfish has damaged the house reef. Activities include windsurfing and there is a small freshwater swimming pool.

Vadhu Diving Paradise
South Male Atoll
Tel: 343976/343977
Fax: 343397

Airport: 8 km (5 miles)

31 cabanas with unheated freshwater showers, 24 with air conditioning. Most of the rooms are in modern two-storey chalets. Sunset Wing offers suites decorated to a high standard straddling the lagoon.

Japanese divers have exclusive rights to this resort and it is therefore difficult to get into. Perched atop the edge of the Vadhu Channel which separates North and South Male atolls, it offers an unsurpassed range of marine life.

The island itself is small and uninteresting but there is a curious floating bar. The beach is not very good but diving is what Vadhu is about and with depths of 1,000 m (3,250 ft) and more, the Vadhu Channel is a divers' paradise where drift diving is the norm. This is an ideal location for those who want to see large fish such as whale sharks and hammerhead sharks, but do not want to be based further afield in the Ari Atoll.

The diving is run by Japanese instructors and facilities include windsurfing, catamarans, parasailing, fishing, sailing and glass-bottomed boat excursions.

Vabbinfaru Paradise Island
North Male Atoll
Tel: 343147
Telex: 77026 VABBIN MF

Airport: 16 km (10 miles)

31 thatch-roofed rondavels with unheated freshwater showers 14 hours a day. There is no air conditioning.

This medium- to upper-range resort has been revamped and is stylish, lively and young at heart. It is French managed and the guests are mostly Italian and Australian. Island-hopping excursions are arranged to the neighbouring islands of Himmafushi, Thulhagiri, Boduhithi and Giravaru, close to some excellent diving sites.

Diving courses are available but the house reef is disappointing, owing to the damage caused by the crown of thorns starfish. There is free windsurfing and catamaran sailing; activities also include sailing, water skiing and Male excursions.

Guide to the Maldives

Veligandu Huraa (or Palm Tree Island)
South Male Atoll
Tel: 343754/343599/343611
Fax: 343886

Airport: 19 km (12 miles)

16 rooms including de luxe bungalows with hot and cold freshwater showers most of the day.

This fairly new resort has a sophisticated air. It is a very small island – just 15 minutes' stroll all round. Should you feel claustrophobic or want a change of scene, there is a wooden walkway linked to Dhigufinolhu. In between these two islands is a further deserted island for those wanting seclusion. Windsurfing, catamarans, water skiing and fishing trips are available.

Veligandu Island
Rasdhu Atoll, North Ari
Tel: 350594
Fax: 350519

Airport: 48 km (30 miles)

55 rooms, some with open-air toilets. There are 8 air-conditioned de luxe suites and 8 air-conditioned water bungalows. All have hot and cold freshwater showers.

This medium- to upper-range Italian-managed resort is basically a long sand spit. It is in a prime location for some of the best diving sites in the Maldives with frequent sightings of hammerhead sharks and occasional whale sharks. Dive cruises use sites around Rasdhu atoll, but boat traffic in this fairly remote region is extremely light.

Windsurfing, catamaran sailing, parasailing, sailing, fishing, island-hopping and Male excursions are available.

Villivaru Island Resort
South Male Atoll
Tel: 343598
Fax: 343742

Airport: 29 km (18 miles)

60 rooms, 31 air conditioned. Hot and cold freshwater showers.

Villivaru is the sister island of Biyadhoo, which is 450 m (500 yards) away across a narrow, deep stretch of water. Like Biyadhoo, it is run by the Taj Group of hotels. It has an air-conditioned restaurant.

The island is a beautiful sight viewed from Biyadhoo but although it is much smaller, it is generally not as pretty. The standard of cuisine is said to be not as high as that on Biyadhoo. However, the house reef and diving are excellent. There are five points on the island which give easy access to the reef for shore divers.

The dive centre is owned by Nautico Watersports Centre, a German company which also has a base at Biyadhoo. PADI courses are available from Beginner to Assistant Instructor. CMAS courses can be arranged if numbers are sufficient. Theory classes take place in the bar or in the open air, with practical sessions in the shallow water in front of the dive centre. Canon, Fuji, Sea and Sea and Hanimex 35 mm underwater cameras are available for hire but you should bring your own film.

Villivaru regularly uses about 20 dive sites on the east side of the atoll. Most of the dives are in channels where most of the marine life is found. Large fish including sharks, manta rays, eagle rays and giant napoleon wrasse are common. Night dives can be made by experienced divers on the house reef. They are also available by boat on nearby reefs, subject to demand. All night diving should finish by 9 pm, as this is the time of the last sitting for dinner. It is normal on occasions for the Villivaru boat to pick up Biyadhoo divers *en route* to the dive site. This can mean a heavy load and not much space on the dive boat.

You should check the dive profile with the divemaster on the boat; once at the site divers quickly disperse.

Other activities offered include windsurfing, catamarans, sailing, fishing, football, water skiing, parasailing, island-hopping and Male excursions. There is also a regular free ferry service between Villivaru and Biyadhoo, should you want a change of scenery.

Ziyaaraiyfushi Tourist Resort
North Male Atoll
Tel: 343088
Fax: As above

Airport: 40 km (25 miles)

65 bungalows. No air conditioning. Unheated saline showers.

Close to Reethi Rah, Ziyaaraiyfushi is a small island which can feel rather overcrowded with a large number of rooms in a small area. Although there is no natural beach and no house reef, the lagoon is excellent. In addition to diving, windsurfing, catamaran sailing, water skiing and fishing trips are available. All diving is by boat.

NOTES

APPENDICES

Helicopters
Useful Addresses
Further Reading

HELICOPTERS

Hummingbird Helicopters offers passengers a swift and efficient transfer service to their resort island, with the most spectacular view of the coral reefs and islands below. Apart from delivering you effortlessy and early to your destination, the helicopter journey will be a memorable feature of the holiday, albeit a slightly noisy one.

Hummingbird is British managed with British crews, and operates Sikorsky S61N helicopters with 25 airline seats and large picture windows that are ideal for photography. The cabin is not pressurised, so you can open the small side windows.

A variety of excursions are offered.

Diving Excursions to Ari Atoll

Clients are flown to Kandolodhu, Hummingbird's uninhabited island where they are met by a *dhoni* already equipped with diving bottles and two diving instructors. They dive at Shark Point and then return to Kandolodhu for a barbecue lunch. In the afternoon they go for a second dive then return to Kandolodhu for the return journey to Hulhule Airport.

Ghatafushi 'Robinson Crusoe' Picnic

This is another excursion to uninhabited Kandolodhu, which leaves Hulhule Airport at 8.15 am. The flight takes just half an hour. At Kandolodhu a *dhoni* collects the clients and takes them on a boat trip to Fesdu Fun Island where they have a drink and look around the island for 45 minutes. They then go on a half-hour *dhoni* trip to the island of Ghatafushi. This is another small uninhabited island with a sandy lagoon and beautful white beach surrounding it. A barbecue lunch is provided and clients can relax for approximately two hours.

They then visit Feridhoo, an inhabited island where a local welcomes them on arrival with a fresh coconut drink, then gives them a guided tour of the island. A direct *dhoni* trip takes

you back to Kandolodhu, arriving at approximately 5 pm, with a Hummingbird flight back to Hulhule Airport.
Price: US$136 per person (minimum eight people per flight).

Ari Beach Away-Day Excursion

Clients travel to the beautiful resort of Ari Beach situated at the southern tip of Ari Atoll. This island has a very beautiful lagoon – one of the largest in the Maldives. The journey takes 35 minutes and the approximate arrival time is 9 am. Lunch in the restaurant is included in the price. Diving can be organised as there is a dive base on the island, but there will be an extra charge for this. The rest of the day can be spent looking around the island, relaxing and snorkelling.
Price: US$115 per person.

Inhabited Islands and Resorts Excursions

There are two choices for this excursion:

1. A twenty-minute flight from Hulhule Airport to the inhabited island of Rasdhu, situated at the northern tip of Ari Atoll. Clients are welcomed with a kurumba (young coconut) drink and then given a guided tour of the island by a local. They then take a twenty-minute *dhoni* trip from Rasdhu to Kuramathi Tourist Resort for lunch, with the rest of the afternoon spent at their leisure on this large island, which is split into three resorts.
2. Similar to the above but the inhabited island on this occasion is Bodu Folodhu which is twenty-five minutes' flying time from Hulhule. Lunch and an afternoon of leisure is spent on the exclusive and beautiful small resort of Nika Hotel, which is a ten-minute *dhoni* trip away.
Price: US$125 per person.

15-Minute Sightseeing Excursions

These excursions begin from Hulhule Airport and fly over the nearby islands in Male Atoll. They give a good view of the

formation of the atoll, the lagoons and the reefs. If time allows, Hummingbird will fly you over the islands where you are staying to show you the view from the air.
Price: US$62 per person.

All these excursions provide an ideal opportunity for some unusual photographs. The 15-Minute Sightseeing Excursion is available on Sunday mornings, although if you have at least 12 people, an alternative day can be arranged. All the other excursions are available on Tuesdays and Thursdays.

For reservations, contact Hummingbird at the address shown under 'Useful Addresses'.

USEFUL ADDRESSES

Government Offices

Ministry of Tourism
F/2 Ghazee Building, Ameeru Ahmed Magu,
Male 20-25, Republic of Maldives.
Tel: 323224/323228

Department of Information & Broadcasting
F/3 Huravee Building, Ameeru Ahmed Magu,
Male 20-05, Republic of Maldives.
Tel: 323836/323839

Ministry of Atolls Administration
Faashanaa Building, Marine Drive,
Male 20-05, Republic of Maldives.
Tel: 322826/323070

Ministry of Trade & Industries
F/1 Ghazee Building, Ameeru Ahmed Magu,
Male 20-05, Republic of Maldives.
Tel: 323668

Department of Immigration & Emigration
F/2 Huravee Building, Ameeru Ahmed Magu,
Male 20-05, Republic of Maldives.
Tel: 323913

Other Organisations in Male

Central Hospital
Sosun Magu, Henveiru,
Male, Republic of Maldives.
Tel: 322400

Flying Swiss Ambulance Clinic
Huvadhoo, Marine Drive,
Male, Republic of Maldives.
Tel: 324508/324509, Telex: 77089 FSA MF
Emergency Tel: 324500 (24 hours)

Hummingbird Helicopters Ltd
Luxwood No 2, Marine Drive-H,
Male, Republic of Maldives.
Tel: 325708, Fax: 323161, Telex: 66185

Dhirham Travels & Chandling Co Pte Ltd
Faamudheyri Magu,
Male 20-02, Republic of Maldives.
Tel: 323369/323371, Telex: 66027 ATHAMAA
(Business: Construction/island suppliers/forwarding agents)

London Addresses

MASTA
London School of Hygiene and Tropical Medicine
Keppel Street, London WC1.
Tel: 071 631 4408

Toni de Laroque ('The Maldives Lady')
UK Representative for the Maldives
3 Esher House, 11 Edith Terrace, London SW10 0TH.
Tel: 071 352 2246, Fax: 071 351 3382

Business Hours

Banks	0900–1300	Sun–Thurs
Government Offices	0730–1330	Sat-Thurs
Shops (Male)	0600–2300	Some do not open Fri am
Post Office (Male)	0730–1330	
	and 1600–1750	Sat–Thurs

NOTES

NOTES

NOTES

NOTES